D1313446

THE VERY SPECIAL WORLD OF THE SHEEPDOG

Tens of thousands of fertile acres of land, all over the world, would be worthless to their owners without the invaluable help of fit, efficient sheepdogs to herd the sheep that graze there. One man and his dog can control a flock of sheep on inaccessible mountains or fells more effectively than the cleverest gadget dreamed up by the brainiest inventor.

This book takes the reader into the world of shepherds and their dogs and describes the mystique of training dogs until their rapport with their master is so close that they can almost steal the thoughts from the back of his mind.

With the shrewd insight and earthy humour for which he is known, Phil Drabble also takes the lid off other programmes, in which he has been concerned in televising wild and domestic animals, some of which have been crowned with success – and others with disaster!

Also by Phil Drabble in Sphere Books:

Phil Drabble's COUNTRY SCENE
COUNTRY SEASONS

One Man and His Dog

PHIL DRABBLE

SPHERE BOOKS LIMITED
30/32 Gray's Inn Road, London WC1X 8JL

Published simultaneously in hardback
by Michael Joseph Ltd and in paperback
by Sphere Books Ltd 1978
Copyright © Phil Drabble 1978

My sincere thanks are due to the shepherds and
their dogs for making this book possible; and to
Philip Gilbert and his team for capturing their pleasure,
excitement and good fellowship with the cameras.
Last, but by no means least, my thanks to Eric Halsall
who was the perfect partner whether things
were rough or smooth.

TRADE
MARK

This book is sold subject to the condition that
it shall not, by way of trade or otherwise, be lent,
re-sold, hired out or otherwise circulated without
the publisher's prior consent in any form of
binding or cover other than that in which it is
published and without a similar condition
including this condition being imposed on the
subsequent purchaser.

Set in Linotype Baskerville

Printed in Great Britain by
Hazell Watson & Viney Ltd
Aylesbury, Bucks

CONTENTS

ACKNOWLEDGMENTS

The author and publishers are grateful to
Derek Johnson for supplying all the photographs
with the exception of number 26, which is
reproduced with kind permission of
Whitehaven News, and to Andy Bloomfield
for his delightful cartoons.

FOREWORD

Phil Drabble has the great and unusual ability to find the perfect words to convey the country scene, whether he is describing the soft colours and the rounded hills of the Lake District, or the intense almost savage stare of a sheep dog as he overcomes a stubborn ewe.

This ability has charmed and captivated not only the readers of his previous books, but millions of television viewers, bringing him friends and followers from all walks of life. Phil Drabble's gift for conveying so exactly wild life and the countryside brings a rare breath of fresh air, sadly lacking in this high speed modern age. No doubt much of it is due to his country upbringing and very practical teaching both by the side of law and order – the gamekeeper, and no doubt as helpfully – the poacher. This background has given him great insight into the minds both of highly intelligent but often quiet and reticent farmers and their canine partners. Through his knowledge he is able to get these countrymen to speak both in the book and in his television programmes with a naturalness and unusual candour.

Those who know his work can only be delighted by this new book, which balances Phil Drabble's knowledge and love of the countryside with his deep feeling and care about broadcasting, and he reveals the problems and frustrations, and the satisfaction and delight of being involved in a new television idea – the BBC-2 *One Man and His Dog* series.

As always, the reader will not be disappointed for

his writing is vivid and has great clarity, and together with his individual style makes this a fascinating book both for the avid country lover and those perhaps less fortunate city dwellers, who get their only taste of the country through books and the television screen.

Philip S. Gilbert

"I looped the loop to the bottom..."

Chapter One

A FALL BEFORE PRIDE

My foot slipped at the top of the stairs and I looped the loop to the bottom. Apart from a sharp crack of protest as my weight landed on it, my forearm stood up to the task of skidding me down as if it had been designed as the runner of a sledge. Gerry Cole, who was piloting me through the maze of passages at Television Centre, side-stepped instinctively. A second ago, I had been following her in line astern. The next time she blinked her eye, I was the limp heap which had nearly swept her off her feet as it passed her on the stairs. 'He's not in *that* much of a hurry,' she said.

'He' was her boss, Philip Gilbert, who was producing the TV series I was working on. He is not famous for dragging his feet, but Gerry reckoned that my precipitate descent was pushing things too far.

It isn't easy to fall down a long flight of concrete

steps and finish up unscathed, but I felt no serious pain. Yet I knew from experience that the air would have been blue with protest if nothing were amiss, because my instinct is to shout loudest when I am hurt least. The fact that my reflex actions hadn't prompted a word out of place was certainly ominous. Gingerly flexing my muscles, I moved my hands and feet and spine to test how many bones were broken. All seemed normal except my forearm, on which I'd skidded down step to step. That was suspiciously numb.

I was due in the studio at 10 a.m. to write and dub the commentary for part of the film we had just shot about sheepdogs. It was to be the first of a series called *One Man and His Dog* which I had been invited to link and present.

A week or so earlier we had been to a remote farm high in the hills overlooking Morecambe Bay in Lancashire and filmed collies herding sheep and a litter of sheepdog puppies, to illustrate the inside story of a shepherd and his dogs. Some of the shots had been synchronised with sound while the shepherd was telling me about his life in lonely places and the dogs that shared it. But a great deal of the first programme in the series was silent film which had to be cut and edited and tailored to time and shape. My job now was to compose a commentary of exactly the right length to fit the edited version and to dub it on the sound track as if it had been spoken when the original film was shot.

It is a testing task when all is well, but I knew that when feeling seeped back into my arm, it might soon become painful enough to sap my concentration. The more time I squandered, the easier it would be to make a mess of the commentary.

Sliding into my studio seat, I gingerly lifted my left arm with my right hand, and laid the forearm gently on the desk beside me. Numbness gave the illusion that it belonged to someone else, so I got on with the job while the going was good. It was a time-consuming process for it can easily take several hours to compose and dub on twenty-five minutes of smooth commentary.

All went well while my arm was resting on the desk but, when we broke for lunch and I had to lift it from its support, the searing pain jerked me back to reality.

I was despatched to the first aid room, where the sister prodded me gingerly, put my arm in a sling and told me to swallow a couple of gigantic pills. The sling gave a soothing support but I was suspicious that the pills might not take kindly to the canteen beer, so I 'palmed' them harmlessly into my pocket.

The third leg of the sister's treatment was even more unwelcome. 'I can't tell if you've broken your arm,' she said. 'Go down to the local hospital right away and have it X-rayed.'

She had to do a report on the cause of the accident so, bored with bureaucratic bumph, I said the first thing that came into my head. 'This young woman shoved me down stairs,' I lied and, as so often happens, the slander stuck. Contributors are now warned that, if they don't bring home the bacon, Gerry Cole will soon decant them from a great height where there is no soft landing!

A couple of pints at lunchtime put thoughts of hospital in perspective. Once in an outpatients department I might be well and truly stuck so that there would be no chance of escaping to put on the commentary that was the purpose of my visit.

My arm was now so painful that I couldn't estimate

the extent of the damage, but I had no intention of becoming a guinea pig at a London hospital. The last thing I wanted was to allow a half-trained student to practise on me before discharging me with an arm shaped like a boomerang. So I supped my ale and returned to the studio with the intention of sticking it out till my own doctor could look at it when I returned home.

Next day, an X-ray confirmed that the arm was broken between the wrist and the elbow and the specialist told me he would have to stick it in a splint. Explaining that we were filming the first of a series of international sheepdog trials next week, I hammered the point that a man introducing it with his arm in a sling would do nothing to promote a relaxing, rural image.

'There is no point in calling yourself a specialist,' I told him, 'if you aren't better as well as different.'

He turned up trumps. He fixed my arm in a rigid right-angle with a tubular splint as thin as a stocking. The only snag was that it was impossible to wangle a jacket sleeve round the elbow so that I feared, at first, that I would still have to hang it in a sling and stick the empty sleeve in my jacket pocket.

However, my tailor slit the sleeve from cuff to shoulder so that it was possible to get my hand through the armhole each morning so that Gerry could stitch the sleeve together over the tubular splint. It was one of the penalties for pushing chaps down stairs! I kept it in a comfortable sling most of the time until it was necessary to appear before the camera. Then one helper heaved my jacket down and another levered my rigid arm up until my hand could just be jammed into the pocket. It was the last half inch that hurt!

However, we recorded the rest of the series of eight programmes without anyone remarking on the fact that I never took my hand out of my pocket!

The idea for the series had been implanted in Philip Gilbert's mind more than a year before. He was on holiday in Northumberland, and visited a local agricultural show. There is nothing 'smart' about such events in the wild hill country of the North. The locals turn up in respectable country tweeds, to gossip and to criticise or, more rarely, to admire the exhibits of their neighbours.

A few urban holidaymakers join them, in denims and the bizarre gear that townfolk delude themselves that country folk wear. Everybody knows everybody else – except the strangers from down south, who can generally be conned for a free pint or so in the bar of the local afterwards!

It was not a good day to enjoy such outings. The glorious hills were only a dim outline, shrouded in mist, and the show had scarcely begun before it was sheeting down with mountain rain. The locals were oblivious. Rain is second nature to such folk. Their tweeds mopped it up or their macs sealed it out, without so much as swilling off their sly smiles as they watched the strangers retire to their cars to pickle their troubles in gin.

Philip Gilbert is made of sterner stuff. He joined the inner circle of enthusiasts watching the Cumberland wrestling. Every bone-shaking fall registered in his mind, every arm-twisting wrench was agony in his imagination. He mingled with the little crowd in the flower tent, eavesdropping on the gossip about winners who bought their specimens from somebody else, and how exhibitors of prize leeks bamboozle the judges. If disgruntled unsuccessful competitors are to be believed, a leek will swell, proud, to twice its natural size if you leave it overnight in a tub of rain-water. And you force the growth of a prize chrysanthemum by watering it with urine from a pregnant mare – or neighbour!

There was a terrier show – for real dogs that earned their keep doing battle underground, driving foxes out to hounds or killing them in single combat if they skulked. None of your raddle-faced, big-bottomed blondes at dog shows like this, kneeling by effete creatures in the ring, holding canine heads up in one hand and tails in the other, lest the judge's eye penetrate their weak points.

Dog owners at such shows are hard-bitten men who can follow hounds all day on foot and care more for killing vermin than making sport with them.

At the top end of the ground, where the arena merged with the foothills beyond, there was activity that had drawn few spectators.

A bunch of weather-beaten men stood at one corner of the field, some holding a sheepdog on a lead, others on a piece of string. About four hundred yards away, five scraggy mountain sheep had bunched together to face the approach of a black-and-white collie. His master, a shepherd, stood close to the arena, conveying his commands partly by whistle and voice and partly, it seemed, by telepathy.

Philip Gilbert stood idly by, not comprehending the finer points of the performance, but marginally interested in the magic of the shepherd's remote control.

The dog kept his sheep bunched and worked them towards his master, coaxing and threatening and driving them between pairs of hurdles, erect as a row of sore thumbs across the field.

Gradually the sheep were brought nearer and nearer to the shepherd until they were driven right round his feet and away to one side of the field. Two of them wore bright red ribbons as a collar.

When the dog had taken them half way up the field again, he made them go through another pair of hurdles, and across the field through a pair on the opposite side. Then they came back to the shepherd, and the dog separated a sheep distinguished by his ribbon collar from his companions, reunited them and drove them all into a 'pen' made from three upright hurdles and one which hinged to complete the enclosure.

The whole exercise was observed by a judge who announced each dog's score as his part in the contest was done. This scoring was such mumbo-jumbo to an outsider that it was impossible to predict which dog was winning, but it would have been an unimaginative dolt who was not spellbound by the rapport between man and dog: As each dog finished, five fresh sheep were let out of the compound, four or five hundred yards away, and the performance was repeated, again and again, till the pattern became as predictable as a ritual dance.

The rain never let up. It seeped into sleeves and down necks and trickled into welly boots, but Philip never noticed it.

His eye is as receptive as a camera lens so that every dog that ran etched itself onto the television screen that lives in the back of his mind. He saw close-ups of adoring canine eyes, watching for the faintest hint from their master that this sheep must be singled out or that rebellious old ewe hustled on a bit.

When things were going wrong he saw the subtle transference of thought that translated the frustration in the man's mind to blind panic in the dog's. And, occasionally, he saw the reverse when a wise, experienced dog retrieved his boss's blunder.

The longer he watched, the more firmly he was convinced that this could make compelling television. The miraculous long-focus lenses of modern cameras would be able to fill the screen with close-ups quite invisible to naked eyes. Sheep may look stupid and as easily managed as moronic men, but the camera is ruthless at destroying such illusions. It would soon disclose the truth that a stubborn, determined ewe can often be more than a match for the most intelligent dog in unison with his master. By the end of the day the foul weather had done nothing to dilute his enthusiasm, but the germ of the idea almost withered and died under the pressure of other work when the holiday was over.

A year later, dredging his mind for future programmes, the sheepdog idea bubbled to the surface once more.

Before putting up the idea for a programme, Philip decided to test his first impressions by having a closer, more objective look. The English National Trials were held that year at Leek, in Staffordshire, on an uninspiring recreation ground, unphotogenic enough to daunt the most enthusiastic photographer. Philip made contact with Lance Alderson, then secretary of the International Sheep Dog Society, who passed him on to the course director, Eric Halsall.

Eric's head is thatched with wool and nobody who had not been suckled on a cade (or orphan) lamb's bottle could possibly be so involved with sheep and the collies that herd them. He eats, sleeps, dreams and thinks sheepdog trials and has forgotten more about them than most of us will ever learn. Almost every weekend in the year, he is watching or helping at a trial and the harder he works at it, the more his enthusiasm bubbles out of every pore.

Philip sat by him, soaking up his non-stop torrent of commentary and background information, but the weather was as foul as the year previously in Northumberland and the scenery at Leek would have been depressing enough in brilliant sunshine.

Philip took some film of his own, for the record, and soon found that the first snag was the sheer scale of the course. The sheep had to be collected – or 'gathered' – from several hundred yards away and 'fetched' in a straight line between two hurdles to where the shepherd stood. They had to be driven in a tight turn round him and guided on the 'drive-away' to one side of the field.

Then they were taken right across the course, through another pair of hurdles in the 'cross-drive', back to a sawdust circle, where a marked sheep was separated or 'shed', when the whole bunch was finally penned in a hurdle sheep pen. A dog lost points if he did not keep the sheep in a straight line from one part of the course to the next; he was not supposed to panic them but had to demonstrate that he was in command by keeping them moving smoothly.

All this took time. Too much time to show in its entirety, if several runs were to be shown on one television programme. And a good deal of the action was too far away to mean much on film. The obvious solution was to edit out the duller bits of the film, leaving in the highlights, but this would not necessarily give a fair assessment of the dog's performance.

One solution would be to put cameras half-way down the course, but the obvious problem was that they might put off the sheep or distract the dogs. Alternatives were to use a scaled-down National course or to film only the latter part of the run. The snag in this, of course, was that a dog that did well early on but lost points while the viewers were watching might turn out to be the winner.

In spite of the weather and the scale of the trials course, the results of the film Philip took were encouraging. Eric's enthusiasm had confirmed his hunch, so he worked out a feasible way of covering it, costed it out, and offered it as a one-off programme, selling the idea of its competitive attraction, the pleasures of watching wonderfully trained collies at work and the sheer professional teamwork between the shepherds and their dogs. The idea was not only accepted by the BBC Planners but they asked for a complete series. This gave the latitude to film a course and competition especially designed for television – provided it had the backing of the International Sheep Dog Society, an attractive location, good weather, a knowledgeable commentator and a suitable 'front man'.

The first hurdle that tripped Philip up was the Sheep Dog Society itself. Philip had seen enough of Eric Halsall and the secretary Lance Alderson to convince him that the result could be delightful. But country folk are deeply – and so often rightly – suspicious of the motives of what they suspect may be bright boys up from the city. Too many television slickers have promised fair treatment to country sports or pursuits or people but ended up by showing travesties under the delusion that they are being smart. Sending-up landowners or portraying country folk as swede-gnawing yokels is always good for applause by the trendies.

The men who frequented sheepdog trials needed no explanation of what goes on, and they had no wish to swell their crowd with strangers addicted to the osculatory antics of professional footballers or the rabble who egg them on. The officials of the Society were extremely cagey, being perfectly happy for trials to remain a friendly participant sport where almost everyone knew everybody else.

Meanwhile, Philip had worked out a format for a series of seven programmes, giving a structure of four heats, two semi-finals and a final. When he costed it out, the arithmetic was encouraging, so he contacted the Sheep Dog Society again.

Lance Alderson and Eric Halsall were extremely conscious of the possible advantages – as well as the disadvantages – of the publicity the sheepdog would get and, eventually, after a great deal of discussion and negotiation, agreement was reached to go ahead. Only at this stage, when there were no official stipulations about who should do the commentary, was it possible to issue an official invitation to Eric to be the commentator. Before the project could be started, his advice was needed about sites for the trials, practicable modifications to the course, and introductions to people in the sheepdog world. In the programmes themselves, he was to develop the competitive angle, using his personal knowledge of competitors and dogs and their individual potential. He was to be the viewers' representative in the judges' tent, explaining precisely why and how the dog had lost the points indicated by the score.

At this point, I was invited to be the front man. I had major reservations. 'Front man' is a term that I detest because it implies what, all too often, it is. A face on the screen, mouthing words that have been implanted in its head by whoever devised the programme, appearing and disappearing at the director's behest as mechanically as a puppet on a string. Apart from the fact that I don't enjoy being pushed around, I had had the uncomfortable experience of being 'front man' once before, about twenty years ago in a series called *The Midlander*. I forgot my lines and could never remember the name of whoever I was introducing next.

Indeed, my memory for names is notorious. Once I have seen a face, it is there for good, but I am so bad on names that my wife and I have had to devise a ruse to disguise the defect. It works rather well.

When a stranger, whose face seems familiar, accosts me when I am with my wife, I greet him like an old friend and yatter trivialities for a while. Then I say, 'Of course, you know my wife.' He doesn't, but my assumption that he does shakes his confidence and he doesn't realise I haven't introduced him to her.

I once had to speak at a meeting chaired by a noble earl and the president of the society took me to meet him first. In deference to his rank, I had put on respectable clothes and, when his lordship himself came to the front door of his ancestral stately home, we discovered our suits were of identical cloth. 'Good God,' he said, 'you've got my suit on!' I've always believed in trading silly answers to silly questions so I said, 'No, I haven't. Mine's pressed.'

He took it very well and we got on fine. When I got home, I told my wife; we giggled about it and forgot it. A year later at the Game Fair, an anonymous man greeted us and I played the old routine. 'Of course, you know my wife,' I said. He obviously didn't, but she chipped in that of course she did and addressed him by name. When he had gone, I asked her how she knew who he was. 'He'd still got your suit on,' she replied.

A memory like that is not the best qualification for being front man to a series about shepherds and dogs. Most of my rural friends are naturalists or farmers or sportsmen. I hadn't a single shepherd of international repute on my visiting list, so the first hurdle would be putting names to faces among a whole gaggle of strangers. The programmes I enjoy are those where I am discussing with friends the things that I know as much about as they do, where I can contribute at least as much as anybody else.

Nor did I have any confidence that a series about sheepdog trials would have much chance of success. I could see that one programme about the work and training of sheepdogs would be fascinating, and another about competitive trials could still hold water. The rugged grandeur of wild hills, with their kaleidoscopic patterns of changing light, could be sheer magic by itself, and the uncanny rapport between man and dog might be a priceless bonus.

But I calculated that, however beautitful the scenery or however intricate the relationships, an endless succession of shots of men, cast in rural moulds, blowing whistles at similar dogs chasing identical sheep through the same hurdles on the same course might prove monotonous long before seven programmes were screened.

I have stayed on the fringes of television for twenty-five years, not because I have done anything outstanding but because I have tried to work for people I like on subjects within my capacity. It is such a competitive game that one failure cancels ten successes and I was far from convinced that the odds on this were heavy enough to make it a viable gamble. So I asked for time to think it over – and went away to do some homework.

Enquiries among friends at the BBC confirmed that Philip Gilbert is a distinguished outside broadcast producer, not famous for backing losers. His successes range from live coverage of rock climbing, such as the ascent of the Old Man of Hoy, to royal broadcasts and the Chelsea Flower Show and the Trooping the Colour right down to the blatherings of Chancellors of the Exchequer on Budget nights. In one month of the 1977 Jubilee celebrations, he had a scanner in Buckingham Palace garden covering the royal procession in the Mall and the return to the palace; a couple of days later, he was involved with a live outside broadcast of the Queen's Progress down the river. The same week, he covered parts of the river pageant and fireworks, Trooping the Colour and the RAF flypast. A few days later, he was involved with the Spithead Review and had a 'live' camera, for the first time, on the Royal Family's private deck on *Britannia*.

His capacity for work was obviously phenomenal and the consensus of my friends' opinion was that I was more than lucky to be asked.

Hatching the plot-sheep style

Chapter Two

HATCHING THE PLOT

Prestigious programmes are supposed to be sired in smart restaurants over expense-account meals which start with smoked salmon and end with port, cigars and a fat contract. I have never had the luck to attend such a function.

The next time I met Philip Gilbert, he was with Eric Halsall in a little pub in Knutsford. The venue had been chosen because it is about half-way between Eric's home and mine. Perhaps it was no coincidence that Philip was already working in the area at the time!

He wanted me to meet Eric, on neutral ground, so that he could assess if we were likely to work together as a team and, if he thought we were, so that he could finally sell the idea to me because I had made no secret of my doubts.

The first meeting with a chap who might have to share the success (or failure) of a programme that one is introducing and linking is always a tetchy time. Both size each other up to see if there are any common bonds or if the relationship, at best, is likely to be purely professional. At worst, it can all too easily degenerate into a state where dislike simmers and bubbles just under the surface so that any bonhomie is no more than a superficial veneer. In any serious business, there is no jealousy like professional jealousy and I have often watched otherwise nice people jockeying for a position to trip up their rivals, only too happy to see them drop a clanger loud enough to scupper their chances of being asked again. It limits the competition in an overpopulated medium.

It was the first time I had met Eric, so we eyed each other warily. I discovered that he is in estate management, and spends most of his working life dealing with farmers and farming problems.

When I walked into the pub, he already had a pint of beer in one hand and a foul old pipe in the other. It turned out to be a characteristic attitude! His weather-beaten face smiles in repose, and his eyes light up at the most oblique reference to sheep and sheepdogs.

A couple of pints and some rough sandwiches later, we'd broken the ice and decided that we could put up with each other. He and Philip had already done so much work looking at possible sites for the trials that they were quite convinced the series would work so that the meeting with me was to try to persuade or coerce me to join them.

Such enthusiasm is extremely contagious and, despite what I still think was my better judgment, we decided to have a go and sink or swim together, a decision I have never regretted.

It was probably a sensible risk for Eric. He had

broadcast on sound radio before but never on television, so he had much to gain and little to lose, but I earn my living with my pen, and I can't afford to tangle with non-starters. Very few people remark if a programme goes all right, but letters pour in by the wastepaper basketful when one makes a bodge of things.

Although I had had no first-hand experience with sheepdogs, the love of any working dog is as much in my blood as it is in Eric's. Tick, my German pointer, is my inseparable companion and she has been on the box with me more than twenty times and complete strangers often stop us to ask if I am Phil Drabble. Flattered in the belief that they must have enjoyed a programme, I straighten my tie and coyly admit that I am. 'Thought you were,' is often the reply. 'I recognised the dog.' However much it cuts one down to size, the fact that a pup one has reared and trained has so obviously made her mark is really as flattering as scoring a hit oneself! I am delighted to bask in her reflected glory.

The sheepdog trials I had watched had all been at too long a range to see precisely what was happening and there had never been a commentator articulate enough to drive the niceties into my head in any case. I said so forcibly, making the point that I couldn't see how repetition was to be avoided, but the other two howled me down. For a few minutes the smile faded from Eric's eyes as he banged the pub table with his malodorous pipe, hammering home hard facts about the thrills and uncertainties of a sport where the nicest people teamed up with the wisest dogs to outmanoeuvre a bunch of bloody-minded sheep.

Philip chipped in with the argument that anyone

normal, who didn't happen to be captivated by the competition, couldn't fail to fall in love with the breath-taking scenery, and it soon became obvious to me that he would be an unimaginative dolt who failed to be infected by Eric's enthusiasm.

The one fly still struggling in the ointment was how long the whole project would take. I live in a pretty isolated spot, a mile from the main road one way and two-and-a-half miles the other. We try to be as self-supporting as we can, so there are always fowls and ducks and geese to be fed, night and morning, and the dogs to be exercised. My wife is always game to cover my jobs as well as her own, but the telephone never shuts up and there is so much VAT and other bumph to cope with, to find bureaucrats something to do between teabreaks, that she has more than enough work of her own. So I try to select work that does not involve being away overnight. Philip said that this series would involve a few odd days filming the first programme at Tim Longton's farm, visits to the farms of other competitors and a solid week probably somewhere in the Lake District for the trials.

The notion of getting seven half-hour programmes shot in a week seemed wildly optimistic. I have worked for plenty of producers who reckon they've done a good day's work if they finish with five or six minutes' usable film. By the time they've messed about and fiddled around deciding what to shoot, it's time for coffee break. Films take time to be changed, there is often something that doesn't work and it takes an hour-and-a-half for lunch because there isn't a pub of the right star rating near enough! The first programme, introducing a shepherd and his dogs, the commands he used to control them and the work they did on the hill, was to be shot on film. That would be done in two days. Three times the output I was used to.

The other seven programmes would be shot on video tape, a medium I had never tried, but I knew it was more like live television, where a number of cameras could shoot what happened, but Philip said he'd explain that later. There were so many potential hazards – from a couple of teeming wet days, to broken gear or a cameraman off the hook – that I was intrigued to discover how anyone with so many successes under his belt gave himself any leeway for hard lines.

'In live outside broadcasts,' he said, 'you're taking risks all the time. You can't control what's going to happen, and you never know if it will happen as the organisers say it will. Even if you are convinced it will do exactly what they say, something unpredictable always seems to turn up. You're never sure that all the cameras will work all the time. They hardly ever do, so you are much readier for risks and geared to re-covering quickly – you hope! – from disaster.'

'You say this is a *calculated* risk,' I countered. 'How did you minimise it or, at least, convince yourself it was a reasonable risk to take?'

'I put my eggs in a lot of baskets,' Philip said, 'to lengthen the odds in my favour. I shall choose a site where the scenery is so good that a lot of people should watch for that alone. I shall make sure of getting the very best competitors, competitors who can talk as well. And I shall break up the monotony – if the trials are as similar as you fear – by interjecting sequences at competitors' farms, so that viewers will feel they know them personally and identify with them.

'I know Eric has experience on sound radio but

27

none on television, so I shall minimise risk with him by making the programme so that he can put most of his commentary on in the studio, after the shots of the trial are edited and finished. If he makes a bodge of that, he can do it again and again, and again – till he does get it right!'

Poor old Eric, I thought. I had had enough of that myself. You sit there, in the studio, with pictures coming up on the screen in the order the script predicts. But talking so that you always finish what you're saying just before the sequence changes seems to get harder, not easier, with practice. There is the producer behind his glass panel, and the sound mixer and umpteen technicians, manipulating film and tape, so that after I have been through the same sequence a couple of times, I always become acutely conscious that there must be hostile eyes behind the glass, resentful at having their time wasted by an incompetent. If I look up, they are talking and joking and, because I can't hear what they say, I am convinced it is at my expense. They might be writing me off as a failure.

But I don't really think it is like that. I think that most people are less than perfect and, in that league, they are such perfectionists that they repeat things, not always because something went wrong on the contributor's part, but often because they weren't satisfied with the quality or timing of a mix. Nevertheless, I began to feel sorry for Eric, who was classed as a risk to be minimised in the studio.

My sympathy was misplaced. Philip's voice etched through my defensive mental shell to explain as gently as possible how he would minimise the risk with me. I soon discovered that I was rated even lower!

'You are the biggest risk,' he said. 'You have got to

28

be in vision to introduce the programme and wind it up, and to talk to some of the competitors. It would be ridiculous to hear your voice but not to see your face so, if it doesn't come off – too bad. But, if I really have to, I can cut the time I use you, either because it hasn't come off or, since it is a new programme, because my initial judgment was wrong. At worst there need be only one-and-a-half minutes of you in vision, which need not be catastrophic in a programme twenty-five minutes long.'

My confidence did not precisely soar. I knew the challenge would stretch me like catapult elastic, but it was disconcerting to realise how close on target he was. I asked him why he'd risked asking me at all.

He said he'd considered lots of professional front men, who introduce daily magazine programmes, but decided that they might err the other way and be too slick. 'I want a programme,' he said, 'with a medium, gentle pace, reflecting the country mood. It has got to be genuine and I am prepared to sacrifice a little professionalism, in presentation, for the credibility of someone who is a real countryman himself, and can speak with authority.'

Luckily for me, he had seen one of the Getaway series on hound-trailing. It had been filmed at Melbreak, near Loweswater, so that the scenery had been superb. Hound-trailing is a participant sport where each man owns and trains his hound to run against the rest, in cut-throat competition. It is a sport as full of strange training diets and mysteries and gamesmanship tricks as whippet racing or cockfighting.

Part of my job had been to talk to a champion trainer, and to persuade him to describe as much of his art as possible. When we got to his house, it was instantly obvious that television interviewers were not among his favourite people! Too many condescending slickers had patronised him before, hoping that viewers would find him 'quaint'. All I could get out of him was a monosyllabic 'Yes' or 'No'.

While the cameramen were setting-up, I tried to chat him up, probing for a common chord. His hounds were in kennels at the bottom of his garden, and scratching about in the yard was a gorgeous duck-wing fighting cock, exhibiting his arrogance to two wheaten hens.

'I like your birds,' I said.

'Birds? What birds?' he replied, peering moronically into a tree overhead. 'I see no birds.'

'That duckwing stag and the wheaten hens,' I said.

It froze him in his tracks and his eyes narrowed. He'd imagined everyone 'from the BBC' was as thick and ignorant as some of them imagined he was. The fact that I not only recognised a gamecock when I saw one, but knew the technical colour, came as a sur-prise. He glowered at me as if I were some sort of 'copper' as well as coming from the city, and asked me bluntly what I knew about fighting fowl.

Delighted to prove his suppositions wrong, I told him that my old man was a doctor from the Black Country of Staffordshire with a lot of miners in his practice. Amongst them was the great Pat Welsh, famous to followers of the illegal sport of cocking, and I said that Pat had taught me much more than I should know when I was young.

'He told me about coming up this way,' I said, 'to stay with a chap called Downy, somewhere near Bolton-le-Sands.'

'Good God, he was my father's cousin,' was the reply, 'and Pat was famous here too.'

Then the trainer started to talk as freely about trail hounds as Pat talked about cocking, only in his case the camera was rolling.

As the years have gone by, a magnum of such acquaintances have blossomed into friends, because I continually meet rural strangers with whom I have a common bond. I knew – and Philip knew – that such previous experiences would throw me into the same fold as many of the men I should meet while filming *One Man and His Dog*. Such countrymen are often natural storytellers, if only one can touch the common bond which is the catalyst.

I asked Philip what stage the programme had reached. He said they'd convinced the International Sheep Dog Society that, treated as he intended to treat it, which was quite objectively, a television series would do their sport good rather than harm. What was most important was that they had agreed to use a course specially designed for television so that more runs could be shown without having to edit out possibly vital sections to squeeze the rest into the available time.

Men, confident enough to risk exposing their failures to a large crowd on a trials field, on the chance that they could exhibit their successes, have to be slightly extrovert. So the chance of starring on the television screen, where millions would be watching, was an intoxicating prospect. Indeed, one of the problems has been that, whatever teams are picked, there will always be some who consider themselves more eligible so that a few pairs of jealous green eyes are often looking in, believing that they could have avoided every pitfall and gaffered – or mastered – every stroppy sheep.

Having obtained official agreement, Eric was the

obvious choice for commentator because it was vital to have a specialist who could convert the jargon into terms that everyone else could understand and, above all, give the reasons why two dogs, apparently of equal merit, had been split into first and second place.

I reiterated my warning that learning wadges of script was not my scene and that I was only happy talking more or less spontaneously. Philip was still prepared to risk it – warts and all! – and that decision tied up the team that was on the hosts' side of the bar counter.

So far as the guests went, it was decided to run a knock-out contest, starting with four teams of four. In the first series, an Irish team was not included, partly because there are fewer working dogs and shepherds up to International class to choose from in Ireland than on the mainland – and partly because the programmes were on a tight financial budget. Touring Ireland to get film of scattered competitors on their own farms would involve considerable expense.

The upshot was that teams were chosen to represent England East, England West, Wales and Scotland. In the first rounds, the teams were recorded competing among themselves to provide four 'National' champions – if you count the winner of England East or England West as 'national'! Two of these winners were knocked-out in the semi-finals to leave two semi-final winners to fight it out for the International Television Trophy.

There were such cries of anguish from the Irish that they had been left out, that the next series was arranged between one team each from England, Scotland, Wales and Ireland, and the Irish justified their bleat by winning the Television Singles Trophy next year with Martin O'Neill, one of the nicest of all the nice people I met in any of the series. He had a wonderfully soft southern Irish brogue with a slow smile that might have cloaked his enthusiasm – if he could have prevented it shining through his eyes!

The only thing not settled by the time they shouted 'Time' in our little Knutsford pub was where the trials would be held.

Philip had decided, in principle, on the Lake District, and he knew the sort of farm he wanted to use. It had to have a relatively flat area – one field, or possibly two – where the course could be laid out, so that there would be no 'dead' ground where dogs or sheep could disappear from the cameras' field of view.

The equipment used would be so heavy and so costly that it would be uneconomic to move the whole lot to an entirely fresh site part way through the series. So it was necessary to pick a site with superb scenery on at least two sides, preferably of distinctly different character. The idea was that part way through the series, the course could be re-positioned because it would be so much easier and cheaper to move a few hurdles than to resite heavy technical equipment. Then cameras could shoot with a background of the lake up to the semi-final stage, and with lovely views of wild mountains to give variety for the rest of the competition.

This ideal farm had to have access for long and heavy vehicles, of up to fifteen tons, but could not be too near a main road, because we didn't want to attract too many of the general public. Recording for television consists of hectic, but short, periods of action, followed by what seem like interminable waits while new locations are set up for interviews or disconnected introductory pieces. Two many people milling around in these inevitably long pauses can be

33

boring for them and frustrating for the crew. What we preferred was that competitors should bring a few family or friends, so that there would be the sort of small knot of knowledgeable spectators who would normally be at such events anyway rather than an urban crowd, decked-out in holiday gear.

Local contacts who knew which farmers were likely to be co-operative – and which not! – and who knew the countryside backwards, were asked to make initial reconnaissances from which to draw up a short list of possible sites. Being used to doing a prodigious amount of 'homework' so that he can talk on better than level terms with people he is directing, Philip did an extended survey himself, seeking out 'possibles' from a large-scale ordnance map and checking them on site.

Then he and Eric visited the most promising locations from the combined surveys, to eliminate any that might have snags for using for trials that had been overlooked when assessing the television practicalities.

Finally, Geoff Lomas was brought in. Geoff carries a hidden magic wand in his hand and, without him, the whole circus would come to a standstill. His official title is Engineering Manager, which is another way of saying that he carries the can for almost anything technical that goes wrong. He encourages or chivvies, as necessary, the gang of riggers and drivers who ensure that cameras and equipment are not only in the right place, at the right time, but have cable connected back to base to transmit the sound and pictures they get.

He organises camera men and sound engineers, electricians and the fuel for trucks. His encouragement is sparse – and well-earned – and his criticism forceful, by any standards. He is equally ready to blast the producer for an unfair demand as he is to berate one of his staff for falling below his standard.

So it is natural that Philip calls Geoff in at the planning stage so that he can share the responsibility of choosing a site where deployment of the equipment is possible. I have no idea if it is standard practice with other producers, but certainly Philip and Geoff go round the final short list and agree the final choice. It is typical of the teamwork which makes the whole caper such a pleasure.

While they were finally making up their minds about the precise spot where we should meet for the trials in September, it was decided to begin work on the series by filming the first programme as an introduction to show viewers what sheepdog trials are all about.

"... they secretly regard sheep, not as cosseted darlings..."

Chapter Three

FARM IN THE FELLS

We started off with Tim Longton. He is country born and bred, with generations of yeoman farming blood in his pedigree. Although he is obviously highly successful, there is no taint of brash modern tycoonery about him; no flashy car, nor chromium-plated cocktail bar.

Tim farms between seven and eight hundred acres in the Pennines above Lancaster, carrying four hundred and fifty dale-bred ewes and a suckling herd of seventy black hill cattle with calves at foot.

One glance at his weather-beaten face and work-worn hands leaves no doubt about the fact that he and his family farm the land themselves. They think nothing of modern, college-trained farm managers with heads full of theory and no experience to back it. They wouldn't pay them in washers. They welcomed me with the courtesy that is the hallmark of such men and we soon discovered that we talked the same language and liked the same things especially dogs.

Ever since I was a kid of eight, I have had a dog at my heels, usually bred specifically for sport. I have owned mongrels and bull terriers for ratting, whippets for rabbiting, and gypsy-bred lurchers, lean as greyhounds and cunning as their owners, for catching hares. Alsatians have (and do!) discouraged uninvited guests and Tick, my German pointer, has been my inseparable companion for years.

I do not suffer fools gladly, either human or canine, so that they have all been well enough trained to win the respect of other doggy men. They form a topic of conversation that soon weaves a common bond between men like Tim and me.

Good manners are still treated as a virtue by such men, so we were taken into the farmhouse for a cup of tea and introductions to the family. As soon as the formalities were over, he was as anxious to get out to introduce me to his dogs as I was to meet them.

The whole family have long been famous for their working sheepdogs and Tim and his brother Tot are still in the very top flight of sheepdog men. Tim's successes in sheepdog trials include the Supreme International Championship in 1966, as well as the English National Championship, a double equivalent to winning soccer's European Cup Final and the FA Cup Final in the same season. He won the International in the class for Farmers' Dogs in 1964 and the English National Farmers' Championship five times.

However important a slice of his life they involve, sheepdog trials are his hobby. He keeps his dogs first and foremost for work on the farm – so, on to the farm we went. Roy, his current champion, came with us.

A stream as bright as gin gurgled down out of the hills towards the farm buildings. The boulders on the shady side, were pockmarked in subtle greys and greens with lichen, and the stones across the ford were treacherously polished.

It didn't look much of a pull up to the sheepwalks above the grey stone house, but it slowed me up in the first half-mile. Tim Longton, lean and wiry, carried no more unprofitable flesh than his iron-ribbed dog, and I reckoned that he would be moving with the same springy shepherd's strides long after sore sinews had seized-up in the back of my knees.

The view from the top was breathtaking. Masses of heather, an old grouse calling across the scree, while the limitless sky echoed to the background music of curlews calling – the wildest and most haunting sound in nature.

To the west, over Lancaster, the shimmering sea of Morecambe Bay melted into the horizon, while down in the valley below us, the grey stone buildings of the farmstead seemed as natural as if they had grown there; they breathed a rare air of security in these shifty times.

We sat silent with the dog for a while, admiring the view, and revelling in the solitude. Although we could look right across to the west, the scree still rose and fell around us in sharp vicious cascades and a bunch of sheep were quietly grazing on the short turf that survived miraculously among the rocks.

'Like to see him work?' Tim said. I nodded.

One second, Roy had been lying at our feet, tongue lolling lazily, eyes brimming with the uninhibited adoration such dogs accord their masters. A flick of the hand transformed him from a languid layabout to a professional athlete.

He sped over the rough and treacherous ground with deceptive speed, looking as if he could keep it up all day. One, two, three, four hundred yards he went, in a gentle arc. Only when the dog had gone past the bunch of sheep that Tim had chosen was he stopped in his tracks, with a single, high-pitched blast on the whistle.

Roy clapped flat upon the ground as though he'd been shot. All we could see was a pair of sharp-pricked ears and the white blaze of his face, looking back towards us, impatient for further orders. Or, to be more precise, for further permission to continue, since his enthusiasm has to be restrained, not goaded.

The next whistle sent him jinking away to the right, swerving, effortless as an ice skater, in order to get the sheep in a direct line between himself and his master. Then Tim clapped him, belly to ground again and, with a quieter note, he set him moving towards the sheep, as stealthy as a cat stalking its prey. Sheepdogs are not the philanthropists you might think. They secretly regard sheep, not as cosseted darlings to be protected, but as fair game to be hunted mercilessly. No elderly sugar daddy, ogling the chorus from the front row stalls, has more thrilling fantasies of conquest than a collie herding sheep. As Tim Longton's Roy crept up on his quarry, ears cocked, tongue avidly licking his chops in anticipation, it was only the civilising influence of skilled training which kept his ardour in control.

Sheep's eyes are so situated on the side of their skulls that their field of vision covers enemies in the rear almost as well as a timorous hare's. The venerable old ewe, which was leader of the flock, lifted her head and stamped her foot in school-marmish petulance as if to ask why this busybody cur had to choose the very moment to disturb them when they had just discovered a rare patch of sweet and succulent herbage. Her companions, alerted by the drumming of her hoof, looked up and bunched behind her.

Roy licked his chops again and sneaked a few yards closer. A younger dog, less able to control his desire, might have blustered too close and set them fleeing down the hill in panic.

It is pointless wasting hard-earned cash to feed sheep on sweet pasture if you allow your dog to chivvy them for his amusement, and run their fat off with your profit. So Roy sneaked a few yards closer and the sheep, annoyed, but not afraid, began to walk towards us at a leisurely pace. When they reached about half an acre of close-cropped turf a hundred yards away, Tim dropped the dog again.

Then, at a different whistle, Roy left his sheep and surged away to the summit of the hill above. There was deep heather there and, as the dog passed through, a pack of eight grouse, probably a family party, exploded all around him and skimmed away to the valley below.

There was another bunch of sheep lying on the hill, which Tim had spotted from the movement of a fly-tormented ear, but the dog was sent on over the brow, to look for any that were invisible even to Tim's sharp eyes.

Within a few minutes, odd sheep were silhouetted against the skyline above us as the dog, working on his own initiative, collected them and sent them on their way towards his master.

When he had rounded-up the last of the stragglers, Roy himself appeared, guiding rather than driving them. He never got them flustered but stood no non-sense. So long as they moved at a sharp walking pace – and kept on moving in the direction he wanted – they needed to fear no harassment. But woe betide the stupid ewe that thought she knew best. The dog dived to intercept her, threatening to snap her heels till she had second thoughts and rejoined her more compliant sisters.

When the sheep were all together in a bunch in the clearing where the first lot were gathered, Tim dropped the dog on the far side of them so that he could walk over to inspect them without scattering them. They would have dashed off if Roy had not been on their far side to keep them under control.

Tim had noticed that one was limping, so he walked gently backwards and forwards across the front of the bunch, pointing with his shepherd's crook. Some parted to the right and some to the left, so he withdrew a pace or so to allow them to rejoin and settle until the one he wanted was at the end of the line.

Roy needed no explanations of what it was all about. He crouched, glaring at them with hypnotic eyes till he broke the nerve of the ewe his master wanted so that she faltered for a split-second of indecision.

'Come on,' commanded Tim and the dog dived between the sickly ewe and her fellows, scattering the majority to spill away down the hillside but isolating his victim from the rest. She tried to dash back to rejoin them but the dog was too quick for her. With threatening fangs, he forced her back so that, when the others had deserted her and escaped up to the pasture, he could drive her safely back to the farmstead for skilled attention.

It was a superb example of a predator 'cutting-out'

a victim from the herd. I have watched precisely the same thing on television when wolves were hunting caribou, wild dogs singling out antelopes in African game reserves or lions feeding on the open veldt. Such exhibitions leave no room for doubt about the civilising effect of the shepherd's training, nor the havoc that could be caused by an undisciplined collie roaming the countryside unchecked.

Although it was obviously so thrilling for Roy to cut-out – or 'shed' – his sheep at Tim's behest, he was his cultured self the moment he'd succeeded. He guided her home soberly, 'penned' her safely in the fold and glanced shyly up to receive his mite of praise.

'That'll do!' said Tim laconically. Some might think it an understatement but it is the nearest that I ever hear a shepherd come to demonstrative congratulation.

An untrained dog can create havoc in the countryside. My neighbour in Staffordshire lambs a thousand ewes, which winter more or less undercover in a sheep yard because the ground is so heavy with clay that it puddles into stolid pudding if sheep or cattle tread it in the wet. As soon as the ewes are lambed, they are turned out into hundred-acre paddocks, fenced with wire netting, so that there is no need for daily dogging them onto fresh ground or collecting them for inspection as Tim is forced to do. But fences, good enough to keep sheep in, are not necessarily dog-proof.

A few years ago, they were raided several times and morning visits discovered bloody corpses, often with udders torn out, ears amputated, rib cages laid bare and entrails trailing across the turf.

The victims were such strong sheep that although foxes probably came to scavenge on the carrion, we were pretty certain that the prime culprit was a dog – or dogs. Relays of us sat up with shot guns or rifles at dawn and dusk but all we shot were a few foxes and carrion crows which were rash enough to come for the pickings.

The real culprits came mainly during the hours of darkness so that it was months before a neighbour caught them in the act. One turned out to be a cross-bred alsatian and the other a border collie that would have made a photogenic pin-up in any shepherd's parlour.

They were hunting as a pair – a throwback, I suppose, to the primeval pack instinct – and, though the alsatian was a fairly easy shot, the cunning collie nearly got away with it. He left his mate to face the music and slipped behind a hedge for cover as deftly as a poaching magpie. Only a superb pot-shot at a diminishing target stopped him in his tracks. Sad as it may seem, there is no cure for a confirmed sheep worrier other than a charge of shot.

I mentioned it to Tim Longton, who agreed that some of the best working dogs are the worst offenders if given the chance. Some are so cunning that butter wouldn't melt in their mouths at home but, if they are left loose at night, they can't be trusted and often go several miles into strange territory before transgressing.

So the golden rule in the countryside is never to leave a dog free to wander on his own – or to grumble about neighbours who shoot him if he does.

When we got back to the homestead, Tim showed me his latest litter of puppies. They were much blunter in the muzzle than Roy, their sire, with far less white about them. Their muzzles would fine out and lengthen as they cast off puppyhood but Tim was glad that they had less white about them than Roy.

Roy is a wonderful working dog, but he is so conspicuous that strange sheep often see him coming from afar and scatter to the four winds. A darker-coloured dog could have sneaked round behind them undetected. In sheepdog trials, where no more than a whisker of skill may separate top class competing dogs, the smallest natural handicap or quirk of luck can spell the difference between victory and defeat.

All puppies are appealing, so Tim and I sat quietly on a straw bale, absorbed by their antics. Animal play is not only for recreation or amusement. It is instinctive rehearsal for the serious business of later life, so we watched them learning to fight, in defence of their territory or conquest of another's. Then one tucked-in its tail and hared off, dodging and weaving, while its brothers and sisters packed-up together, hunting it around the straw bales and corn sacks in the yard.

The boss pup of the litter came up at one side of it and spun it off-balance with a deft nudge that allowed its pursuers to close in and grip it by the throat and belly and legs, and it disappeared beneath a tugging mass of excited little hunters. A second later, it broke free and this time was the leader of the pack while another pup played the role of quarry.

All innocent fun, of course, and a delight to watch, but it did drive home the message that collie dogs are not the cuddly paragons that tradition pretends. They are as much predators at heart as wolves or foxes, and it has taken countless generations of domesticity to harness their talents by training and selective breeding.

As we watched them play, it slowly dawned on me that their instincts really had been channelled to an incredible extent. They tired of mock battles and chase-me-Charlie hunts and, as the pace slowed down, one detached itself from its fellows and began to stalk the rest with infinite caution. At first I thought it was still 'hunting' them, but in a more relaxed, catlike manner than the previous exercises in pack law. Then I noticed that its head was extended so that it was staring at them with the hypnotic 'strong' eye of a collie herding sheep. Instead of a test of brute force and agility, this game was a battle of wills and the puppy was trying his hand at driving and controlling his litter mates, precisely as he would herd a bunch of stubborn sheep, in partnership with the shepherd, when he grew up to be a working sheepdog.

Shepherds have a much better chance than strangers of picking the best pup in a litter. They know the characters of the parents and can often spot which looks the most dominant pup likely to be a chip off the old block, and which are the shy and weakly ones. But, equally often, pups are late developers and it is fatally easy to sell the pick of the litter and keep one that would well have gone to strangers.

It reminded me of other examples of the effect of generations of selective breeding in puppies I have owned myself. I was brought up in the Black Country of Staffordshire where bull terriers were illegally matched to fight in the dog-pit as late as the 1950s. Growing up with colliers and ironworkers, who loved fighting dogs and fighting cocks, it was natural for me to have a Staffordshire bull terrier myself because they were superb for ratting, which is a sport I love. It was not uncommon for a litter of these puppies, bred from generations of fighting parents, to start a play-fight at a few weeks old which, if left to themselves, could turn into the real thing and they would sometimes carry on and kill each other.

The gentler traits are just as clearly stamped into a breed by clever stockmen. Tick, my German pointer, was 'pointing' at bumble bees at four weeks old. It was, I suppose, pure play to her to lift a front paw and freeze into rigidity at anything that looked or smelled or sounded interesting. But it was just as serious a rehearsal for her final function in the shooting field as a bull terrier's mock battles or a collie's obsession with anything he could herd like sheep.

Seeing my interest in his puppies, Tim Longton offered to introduce me to an older pup of which he had high hopes. Dot was only a few months old, had passed through the kindergarten playful stage and was about ready to start serious work.

A flock of farmyard ducks was dibbling in the paddock by the house and Tim allowed the pup to wander in their direction. The instant their movements caught his eye, the pup's ears cocked and every muscle in his body tensed. One second he had been a sloppy, playful whelp, the next he was poised to chase, split off a victim from the flock and hunt it to destruction.

Generations of selective breeding had blunted the edges of his savagery so that it was a toss-up whether his natural instinct would be sublimated by the training that so many of his ancestors had received from man. For a nailbiting eternity he quivered with indecision – and then the collie in him won. Dot sneaked off in an arc to reappear at the far side of the birds. An old drake spotted him and hissed a warning to make his harem bunch around him and the young dog used their momentary distraction to creep a little closer. A duck, more panicky than her staid relations,

46

quacked, recoiled from her 'attacker' and her panic was instantly contagious. They all quacked such abuse at the dog that the temptation to quell the riot was too much for him and he darted into the centre of the flock, scattering them to the winds.

Tim blew his whistle till it seemed his eyes would fall out, and the dog subsided as if it had been shot. The first thing to teach a pup of any breed is to come when called, and the second is to drop, or lie down on command. A single blast on the whistle, or through forked fingers, is the shepherd's language for 'Whatever you are doing, don't! *Lie down*, instead.' A trained dog, whether he is coming or going, walking or running, will react to the shrill note as a pure reflex, dropping first and analysing the reason afterwards.

Tim's pup's basic training had been nothing if not thorough so, in spite of the temptation of the foolish flock exploding about his ears, the urgency of that whistled command dropped him in his tracks.

His boss left Dot lying there to cool off, while the frightened birds regained their composure. They are the most stupid creatures imaginable, and Jess my wife, who is normally kind and soft-hearted, gets closer to losing her cool when she goes to shut them up at night than at any other time. Most of them are fairly easy, but there is usually an odd rebel which can be incredibly thick-headed and stubborn. She often says she would like to shoot the last one in or to leave it for the foxes as a lesson to the rest!

When Tim's flustered flock had settled down and the pup had cooled off again, he gave it a signal to come on.

This time, hereditary skills supplemented basic training. The young dog waited for the birds to re-

47

treat cautiously from him and then he slunk behind them at a few yards' distance. If one veered slightly, to right or left, the collie swung the same way, smoothly as if he were the bob on the end of a pendulum. But he didn't weave about more than was necessary, so that he drove the birds placidly across the open paddock with a skill that would have dyed my wife green with envy.

Tim knew that it was important for the puppy to end up feeling that he had won. He knew that if he tried to push them closer to us than they considered safe, they would erupt and panic off in all directions. That could cancel out all the pup's good work by sapping his self-confidence.

So, judging the birds' mood to a nicety, he made the dog drop so that the little flock was bunched at a comfortable distance between him and us. Then he called the pup towards him to receive his reward. 'That'll do,' he said and gave him a perfunctory pat.

The whole demonstration had absorbed my mind to the exclusion of everything else. Selective breeding, which can make pointers point or terriers chase everything that moves by the time they are a few weeks old, is really harnessing instinct to work for man. To breed-in inhibitions is very different. I had just watched a sheepdog puppy enjoying the fantasies of hunting almost to the point of execution. To fetter this urge with restraint that channelled his desires at the last instant, from destruction to protection, seemed almost uncanny.

It was obvious that the pup had no fear of a good hiding because he enjoyed himself so much. The control was mental, almost telepathic, as Tim's gimlet eyes spiked the impulse to hunt almost before it flickered through his young dog's mind.

The man's concentration was impressive and, once he had started the pup on his course, all else was forgotten. As I watched the drama unfold, everything else passed from my mind too. The last thing that worried either of us was relating what we saw to the television screen.

Not so Philip Gilbert. He was less worried about philosophic theories about the dog's mental affinity with man than about the practicality of converting the whole sequence into compelling drama on the box. While I had been lost in admiration for the control the shepherd exercised on a dog, which was far enough away to be immune from instant retribution, he had been attracted by the visual possibilities of a crystal mountain stream.

'Could a dog be persuaded to drive the sheep into view over the skyline near that stunted, wind-wracked tree? And could he bring them down where the slope is not easy, but dramatically steep? It would be nice to see them hesitate, for a moment, before splashing through the turbulent water, and continuing along the stream bank into the kindly shelter of the grey stone farm buildings.'

'All of these things are not only possible, but simple,' said Tim. But he'd only heard the half.

One of the main differences between amateur and professional film-makers occurs in the editing. I always cower at invitations to spend an evening looking at 'marvellous' film. A succession of boring pictures of precocious brats, or quart-sized women crammed into pint-sized bikinis. The only consolation is the hope that they will remain anonymous strangers.

Such disconnected shots are often joined together by a film splicer in whatever order they happen to untangle themselves from the reel, so that the finished product jerks and lurches from subject to subject with neither theme nor sequence.

Film should flow smoothly from its logical beginning to the end and each shot should merge with the next to imply continuity. If one shot shows the dog coming towards the camera, and the next is a 'cutaway' of the shepherd watching it, it is possible to rejoin the action, seconds later, with a shot, taken from behind, of the dog and sheep moving away from the camera. The whole sequence will then appear to be continuous and complete, and the fact that several hundred yards of action have been cut out will not be obvious.

This can be accomplished by filming the whole sequence with two or more cameras simultaneously, and by cutting from one camera to another. An even simpler way, if the sequence can be repeated, is to film it once coming towards the camera, and then again, over the same ground, going away. With the aid of odd cutaway shots, to cover the breaks, it is then possible to tailor the film to the exact desired length.

To do this effectively, each shot is identified by an assistant cameraman holding a numbered clapperboard in front of the camera immediately before or after shooting each sequence. The producer's assistant keeps a record of these numbers and writes an exact description of everything which will appear in the sequence.

Philip Gilbert's assistant is Gerry Cole. Like most career girls who really make the grade, she is completely and utterly dedicated to the job. High-powered women, who battle to the top, are normally too tough for my taste, so my first impression was that I could easily manage without her, and it wasn't vital to be clairvoyant to deduce that the feeling was mutual.

We all stayed in the same hotel, a few miles from Tim Longton's farm, and she came down to breakfast with a visionary look in her eyes, oblivious alike of tepid porridge or scalding coffee, because her mind was far away, fixated on detail she was ruthlessly determined that Philip should not overlook. She was scrupulously polite, encased in a hard crust of professionalism, which convinced me that she regarded me as a tiny cog in the intricate mechanism that she was determined should create a good programme.

So long as I revolved smoothly, as well-oiled cogs should do, I felt she might just tolerate me but, should I make a boob, I was in no doubt that the chilly atmosphere, though still polite, could easily be lethal.

On the first two days, filming at Tim Longton's, we eyed each other warily. I was more flippant than the professional linkman she was used to but I was acutely aware of her critical gaze and lack of comment, whether things went right or wrong. When I fell down the studio steps the next time we met at Television Centre, I could see that I was not living up to her high standards!

It took some time for these first impressions to wear away, but I gradually discovered that the real Gerry, beneath the professional façade, is one of the nicest, warmest-hearted wenches it has been my good luck to work with. She is capable of directing and producing programmes in her own right and what I had taken for brusque disdain is really a cover to cloak her shyness. Now the ice is broken – and it took quite a long time! – we get on famously, and I know nobody I would rather have as an ally in a tight spot.

While I had been day-dreaming about the bond

between shepherds and their dogs, she and Philip had roughed out a plan to film what we had seen. The crew consisted of a cameraman and his assistant, a sound engineer, lighting man, and Simon Betts who was the stage manager.

It may seem odd to have a stage manager to film on a remote hill farm in the Pennines but the camera may be hundreds of feet, or even yards, away so that the producer is out of touch with whoever he is filming. So a stage manager, with walkie-talkie radio, stage manages the action by relaying instructions from the producer.

The first shot was to establish the fact that I had gone to a hill farm, to meet the owner, his dogs and his sheep. There were long discussions about skylines and angles, which farm buildings were most photogenic, and precisely where Tim and I were to appear so as to sketch in the whole situation most economically. It took about half an hour to set-up that first sequence, position the camera and fit Tim Longton and me with radio microphones.

The microphones were pinned to our shirts, the transmitters secreted in our pockets and aerials down our trouser legs, to transmit our conversation to the sound recordist's tape recorder without clumsy cables connecting us.

While everyone else was messing about, Tim and I sat on a straw bale comparing the merits of our favourite breeds of dog. I mentioned that Tick had a natural ability for herding things and I wondered how many such common factors there were between different breeds of working dogs. It had so happened that a new neighbour had caused incalculable damage to my wildlife reserve by allowing his keepers to kill my badgers when they crossed the boundary from my land to his. War had broken out between us and I discovered that, when a flock of his young pheasants strayed into my wood, Tick would round them up, as a sheepdog would, and drive them over to the other side of my wood where they settled down instead of going back.

This was not strictly illegal since pheasants belong to whoever happens to own the land they are on at the time, but it was thoroughly reprehensible! But lots of countrymen consider that no holds should be barred in such battles of wits, and the story established a common bond between Tim and me which helped us work together as friends instead of stiff acquaintances.

It launched him into stories of the 'strong eye' in sheepdogs – many of which have a dash of pointer or setter blood in their pedigree – which makes them cast wide in search of sheep on the hill and stare-out the stubborn ones when the shepherd wants one separated from the flock. The snag, of course, is that a dog with too strong an eye may almost hypnotise his sheep and, in so doing, grow so intoxicated with his own willpower that his master has a job to get him on the move again.

Television has a very high ratio of 'wait about' to 'do'. As a contributor, I was required to take part in a sequence, perhaps of only two or three minutes' duration, after which it could be an hour or so before the producer was ready to shoot the next sequence. The interval was spent kicking one's heels because most of almost every day was spent setting-up, or moving gear to the next location, in order to shoot relatively short sequences. When at last they were ready, Tim and I felt like old friends, far better able to wander naturally around his farm than the strangers we had been a few hours before.

We went up the hill to watch two of his dogs working together as a brace, rounding-up sheep from the sharp stone scree just below the skyline. One dog swung in an arc round one edge of the pasture while the other checked that no sheep escaped attention on the other side. Each dog had been taught different commands for the same exercise so that they could be started and stopped or swung left or right independently. It was an uncanny demonstration of rapport between man and dog, especially when one dog was stopped to hold the bulk of the sheep in a bunch, while the other was sent back to comb the countryside for stragglers.

Philip plotted his photogenic course, asking for the sheep to be brought down this gully or that, or positioned so that they made dramatic silhouettes against the horizon. Notes on Tim's whistle, no more than high pitched mumbo-jumbo to our untutored ears, obviously spelt out precise commands to the dogs. The mass of bleating woolly bodies came direct for the camera, passed on each side, engulfing it momentarily, before passing on down by the rippling stream to the farmstead, leaving the rank stench of warm wool hanging on the air.

When they had got as far as Philip wanted, he told Simon Betts, over his walkie-talkie, to get Tim to hold it for a moment, while cameras were repositioned. Then he asked him to return the sheep to their grazing up the hill. Gerry continued scribbling on her clipboard till she had the shot documented to her satisfaction, before leaving us to go down to the cars behind the barn. She returned, long before I realised what she was doing, with a huge flask of coffee, cardboard cups and biscuits. Producer's assistant covers a wide range of virtues!

There would be quite a pause before the sheep had dispersed over their grazing ground again, so we filled the time with our coffee break and re-siting the cameras before repeating the shot from a new angle, from which the two sequences could be edited and mated into a complete story of dogs collecting the flock from the hill and bringing it to the homestead.

Quite a while was spent establishing the fact that I had gone to visit Tim at home. We walked together from the house across the yard, ending with him introducing me to his champion dog and explaining the physical points he looks for in a working dog. Easy and simple as this may sound, it took us half an hour or so to accomplish. We had to have the right background, and walk just far enough for a snatch of conversation to establish which voice belonged to which. Since neither of us claims to be an actor, we never said the same thing twice, so were either talking when we should have stopped, or had finished before we got there. So we had to do it again.

Then the whole caper was repeated while we watched and discussed the pups playing, but the really gripping part came (almost literally) when Tim demonstrated working with a less than half-trained dog which was not yet under proper control. He deliberately set out to show something that could go badly wrong. It was a most courageous thing for a man with an international reputation to risk making a fool of himself before a television audience.

Dot, the pup, began to work a bunch of five sheep and did so well at first that I feared it would make the whole process look deceptively easy. Then, as so often happens, one sheep began to play up and the bunch split. The temptation was too much for the pup which was on the very point of diving in to settle matters by gripping the culprit in his jaws. Tim raised his crook and out-dived the diving dog, dashing between them and holding them apart, not by blows – as some shepherds would have done – nor even by harsh words. He kept them apart only by the shadow of his threatening crook and sheer concentration. It was a battle of wills that I shall long remember.

During most of the demonstration, the camera had been behind Tim, looking over his shoulder at the sheep and the dog, which was obviously keener to eat them than herd them! Just for a few brief seconds, he had had to desert his command post to dive between dog and sheep to prevent a bloody catastrophe. What was captured on the film was the shepherd's-eye view of the whole thing but, since it was shot over his shoulder, it was impossible to see what Tim's reactions to near disaster were.

Philip would like to have repeated the whole sequence, getting a sheep's view of the shepherd so that he could cut between the two shots, discarding enough film to bring it down to the length he needed. It was obviously impossible to repeat, but Philip did want Tim's eyes to look over the camera and follow where the sheep had been.

Simon Betts, the young stage manager, was cast in the role of harried ewe. He crouched low, weaving back and forth exactly as the sheep had done. To outsiders, the whole pantomime must have looked ridiculous, for one grown man was cavorting about on all fours, pretending to be a sheep, while the shepherd put on an act of threatening the equally imaginary dog that was yearning to run amok. The rest of us were rolling about in uncontrollable mirth but, to

56

their credit, the two star performers took the charade seriously. When shots of Tim's menacing eye were edited into film of the genuine drama between dog and sheep, it looked perfectly natural.

Finally, Tim demonstrated the commands he used to control the working of his dogs. Watching them work, it is tempting to imagine that a sophisticated vocabularly would be necessary to produce instant obedience in such an infinite variety of circumstances. The fact is that he used only four different commands to make a dog complete the whole elaborate ritual. 'Walk on' sends the dog away from him. 'Go left' or 'Go right' establish direction. When the dog has been 'aimed' to one side of the sheep, he will go on until he has passed them and either 'Go right' or 'Go left' will bring him behind them so that they are between the dog and the shepherd. The next command, 'Walk on', will bring him towards the sheep, this time back towards the shepherd. The only other command necessary is to stop.

That, of course, is an oversimplification since an art so ancient is naturally wrapped in mystique. A shepherd never does say 'Go right' or, if he does, I've never heard him. He says 'Away to me', which the dog interprets as go to the right. And, when he wants him to swing back and move left, he says 'Come bye, now, come bye'.

Watching border collies work is like sitting in a London pub, listening to rhyming slang. It took quite a time for the meaning to percolate but, as soon as the meaning dawned, I was instantly transported from the spectator's aloofness to the inner circle of a participant sport. It produced a cosy glow of one-up-manship over the crowd of strangers still mystified by the jargon.

To drive the sheep away or, having manoeuvred to the far side of them when the same command brought the dog towards his master, he was simply told to 'Walk on'.

'Look back' sent the dog back to check that he had not overlooked a sheep in gullies or dead ground behind a boulder or lying-up in bracken or rank heather. 'Stand', 'Lie down' or 'Sit' were self-explanatory, though each shepherd varies slightly in the way he trains his dog.

The snag, in voice commands, is that the human voice is thrown about in cascades of echoes by the cliffs and valleys of hill country so that, at first, it is distorted and then dissipated by the distance.

So shepherds duplicate their voice commands by a system of shrill whistles which carry further in rough terrain. Some produce a piercing note by putting two fingers into the mouth, in the shape of a V, and placing the tongue against the finger tips.

It was an art I mastered as a lad, useful alike for calling my dog or attracting the attention of local wenches whose ears were attuned to such wolf whistles. Although frowned-on by the family as being very 'common', I have always regarded such virtuosity as being one of my few social graces.

Shepherds regard such medleys as invaluable assets. They are capable of almost infinite variations on each theme so that it is possible to produce a different response from different dogs to notes that sound almost identical to human ears. When Tim had two dogs working a flock of sheep at the same time, it would have been useless if both dogs started together, went left or right together and stopped simultaneously. By training each to a slightly different whistle, he could stop one while the other went right or left and then, when he had the flock moving where he wanted, he could keep them bang on course by a separate whistle code for each dog. Not only that, he could also make them work faster and hustle or slow down to the merest hint of movement simply by giving commands with greater or less implication of urgency. The range and mood such notes conveyed were almost infinite compared to the stilted vocabulary imposed by human language. If the dog is sold, the new owner has to learn the commands used to train him.

Unfortunately, not everyone can whistle on his fingers. One venerable old patriarch had such ill-fitting false teeth that they emulated a boomerang each time he tried. He had surmounted the difficulty by buying a metal whistle specially manufactured for the purpose. It was just a piece of tin, folded over, to fit into the mouth, with two holes pierced, one over the other, so that when the user blew it, a shrill note was emitted. Or that was the theory. I tried it without producing more than a salivary gurgle and, when I stopped blowing to cough, it almost lodged on my larynx.

A few weeks earlier, I had happened to visit a little factory in the back streets of Birmingham in search of decoy whistles for fooling foxes into thinking that a rabbit was in its last throes out in the open so that I could shoot the fox when it ventured out in search of my free-range hens. I discovered that the factory made nothing else but whistles, ranging from bosuns' pipes to 'silent' dog whistles. There were contraptions designed to sound like crows or owls or oyster catchers; goose calls and hare calls, policemen's whistles and whistles designed for quelling the natives of darkest Africa.

There were whistles for referees at football matches and the factory owner assured me that some of them were so choosy that they came specially to try a range – which seemed identical to me – because they liked to choose one that 'had the right acoustics' for the ground where they were hired to instil some semblance of discipline into the players. The mental picture of a prima donna, in short pants, raising the echoes of downtown Brum to decide which whistle could best be heard by Aston Villa and which by West Bromwich Albion, boggled my mind.

Perched proudly among such specialised ironmongery were shepherds' whistles made from metal and plastic. When I requested a demonstration of this pastoral instrument, I was gratified to discover that I was not alone in being unable to summon up a note. The manufacturer couldn't either!

But the best whistle of all came in the second series of the Television Trials. Tim Flood was an Irishman who both looked and sounded the part. He had a delightful Irish brogue, and eyes which were always merry though his whistle almost blanked them out each time he called his dog. I thought, at first, that it was just part of his irrepressible sense of fun, a joke to see if we were fools enough to fall for it. Not a bit of it. Tim's whistle was an extraordinary instrument with a vertical cup shaped like a mould to cast a replica of a human nose. Not only did this cup fit, snug as a sheath, over its owner's nose, it was only activated when he expelled air from his nostrils. 'A proper Irish whistle,' I told him, and his eyes twinkled as he gave a tasteful rendition of 'When Irish Eyes are Smiling' to prove it really worked. He rounded off the performance with an exhibition of dog control that would not disgrace any international competition, though I shuddered to think what would happen if he had a cold!

"...a dog with a weak eye..."

Chapter Four

SHEEPDOGS, ANCIENT AND MODERN

It had taken two days' filming at Tim Longton's to
capture the shots that Philip wanted for his introductory programme. Tim, a trials competitor of international standing, had shown us his dogs at their
normal daily work managing sheep on the hill. He'd
introduced us to a litter of pups, still young enough
to be faultless and fill him with high hopes; and he'd
produced Dot, the young dog just ready for training,
so that we could watch his reactions the first time
he was allowed to shepherd sheep. If only his keenness could be harnessed for love instead of war, he
was brimming over with promise. It was a big 'if'.

When this silent film had been edited, I was to go
to London to dub commentary onto it, and that was
when I had fetched-up in a heap at the foot of the
stairs.

Eric Halsall had not been needed for this filming
on the farm. We wanted to establish Tim Longton

with viewers so that he could introduce them to his collies and show how he trains and works them and how indispensable a really good dog is on any farm, especially on hill farms where sheep would otherwise be unmanageable. Eric's turn would come when we needed specialist commentary to explain the finer points of sheepdog trialling.

It took more than that to keep him away, though! Almost every weekend of the year he is watching trials, judging trials, or building trials courses. He takes odd days' holiday to attend directors' meetings of the International Sheep Dog Society – and goes to work in his spare time! So it wasn't likely that a BBC crew would be filming sheepdogs without Eric turning up to see fair play. He did screw up his will power to banish himself for most of the first day, but telephoned from work to see how it had gone, and joined us in the evening.

Apart from then, the only time I'd met him was in the little pub in Knutsford, but we fell into mental step as if we'd known each other all our lives. Whatever their function, working dogs have much in common. It doesn't matter if it is a gun dog or terrier, sheepdog or whippet, it must have discipline and specialised training to bring out the best in it. So all natural handlers of working dogs speak the same language.

At first, Eric was defensive about my suggestion that no dog is a worse sheep worrier than a rogue collie left loose at night – except, perhaps, two rogue sheepdogs, because working together brings out their primeval instinct, and this incites them to hunt as a pack and to separate a weakling from the flock. As excitement grows the killer urge takes over until a couple of nice-natured, well-disciplined dogs revert to brutes as primitive as wolves.

Eric grasped the word as the straw to keep faith in his favourite dogs. 'Wolves,' he said, 'of course. Domestic dogs are descended from wolves and have been moulded by training and selective breeding into our best friends. But their basic instincts are never far from the surface, any more than ours are.'

I wasn't sure if he was right about dogs being descended from wolves – but there are lots of people I should love to clobber with a club, so I conceded that my own brand of civilisation is pretty superficial. Before I retrained my guns on sheep-worrying dogs, he'd changed course onto the history of 'his' breed.

'Primitive man did not need dogs to herd his flocks,' he said, 'so much as to guard them. Wolves and bears and rustlers were more likely to decimate sheep numbers than straying or odd accidents. In some parts of the world they still are. So ancient man bred huge fierce dogs, similar to our mastiffs or alsatians or Pyrenean Mountain dogs, or modern Russian Owtchers. They had to be strong and brave enough to tackle all intruders.'

The significant thing is not that ancient man was clever enough to teach old dogs new tricks. Instead of *teaching* them something new, he simply exploited and adapted their natural instincts to serve his purpose. Most animals – including ourselves – are slaves to a 'peck order' of some kind or other. Children are subject to some sort of discipline because parents and teachers are large enough and strong enough to enforce it, if necessary. Big boys, of all ages, bully smaller fry. But, deep down in most of us lies the rebel urge to try it on. There was certainly no sport I loved better than 'ragging' a wet school gaffer.

64

Tick, my pointer, who is normally a paragon of good behaviour, senses the fact that I am not concentrating on her the moment I grow absorbed in conversation with a guest. Then she will slink slyly off to amuse herself instead of hanging around to do my bidding. In wild dogs and wolves, order is enforced by the pack leader, usually virile enough to take the best bitches for himself and to subdue in battle any rival that disputes that Might is Right. Younger animals in the pack are ever watchful for signs that the leader is past his peak and, the instant one of the contenders senses that he has a chance, he will do battle to try to take over the leadership.

Coupled with the instinct to establish dominance by a leader is an equally strong instinct for submissive behaviour by the subservient members of the pack. If an adult dog growls fiercely at a puppy, it will roll, grovelling, on to its back, exposing throat and belly undefended, as a sign of acceptance of the other's superiority. But if a common enemy approaches and the leader shapes-up to see it off, the whole pack will rally aggressively to help him tear the stranger to pieces.

Middle Eastern shepherds walk before their flocks when leading them to new pastures, so it is likely that the flocks of the Old Testament were accompanied by *guard dogs* rather than collies, which is suggested by Job's moan about men who held him in derision: '. . . Whose fathers I would have disdained to set (upon) with the dogs of my flock' (Job 30.1).

These early guard dogs were chosen from the leaders of a pack. Singly, they were often unreliable because there was always the chance that they might size-up their adversary, decide that he was dominant and exhibit submissive signals instead of attacking him. Once in a pack – even a 'pack' of two – their behaviour sank to the level of cowardly louts who become a dangerous mob when they act in unison. Every burglar knows that, while it is sometimes possible to establish mental dominance over a single guard dog, it is far more risky to enter a compound with two which are liable to gang up on him.

Eric Halsall confirmed that, when wolves disappeared from the British Isles, the emphasis shifted from guard dogs to sheepdogs. He said that a Dr. Johannes Caius had published a treatise, in Latin, called *De Cannibus Britannicus*, which was translated into English about 1570. It described the shepherd dogs of that time which were not very large, because they no longer had to cope with bloodthirsty wolves. They were trained to bring wandering sheep to their master 'whether they heard his voice, or he wagged his fist or whistled at them'!

Nobody seems very clear about the real origin of the word collie, though one school of thought claims that it means black (or coal-y) and another that it means faithful, from the Welsh word *coelio*, to trust. Shakespeare seems to favour black.

Swift as a shadow, short as any dream,
Brief as the lightning in the collied night.

Certainly, in my day, coalminers were both black and known as *colliers*! Equally certainly, a majority of the best Border collies are both predominantly black and wonderfully faithful. So take your pick.

Whatever their origin, collies are trained to shepherd sheep as much by exploiting their instinctive urge as any guard dogs are.

This is where the Welsh word *coelio*, for faithful, seems quite as significant as coaly – or black. A faith-

66

ful dog is a submissive dog, at least towards his master, and in canine eyes the shepherd is the psychological substitute for pack leader. When his master has made him comprehend what it is he wants, it will be the dog's pleasure to comply as a reflex action. That is always supposing that everything goes according to plan!

The snag is that, although some puppies will 'herd' instinctively in play before they leave the nest, they cannot be allowed to try out their skills on sheep for many weeks or months. A stubborn ewe can be a formidable opponent and, if she takes it into her obstinate head that she is going in a particular direction, it takes a powerful and determined dog – a real leader of the pack – to stop her. In addition to that, agile hill sheep can run so fast that no pup will overtake them unless he is sharp enough to pick up a rabbit on home ground, and even gypsy lurchers can't do this before they are more than six months old. To try out a young dog on such mountain sheep before he is physically capable of controlling them would be as stupid as putting a young terrier pup down a hole to a fox before he was old enough to avoid a good hiding. Any intelligent dog, in either case, could be put off for good as effectively by being bowled over by a stroppy ewe or by feeling inadequate because he can't catch her, as if he had been thrashed to prevent him following his instinct.

Eric told me that this is what does, in fact, happen to far too many sheepdogs. When they have been weaned, they are left to run wild about the farmyard and buildings for a few months until they are old enough, and physically strong enough, for training to commence. A characteristic that puppies have in common with human brats is that it is usually the most intelligent which get into the worst mischief if they are left with time and opportunity on their idle hands.

A great many hill farmers are unimaginative men. The height, and often the stony nature, of their land makes ploughing impossible and corn stores unnecessary, so that the farmstead rarely has any substantial buildings to spare. Enough poultry to supply the house are usually kept in a ramshackle corrugated iron shed with a dirt floor, slimy with accumulated dung. Good enough for hens to roost in and, with luck, lay in, but no more than that. So most farmsteads have a small flock of mongrel hens scratching for their living around the house and muckheap.

The dogs fare little better. I have seen Trials winners, worth hundreds of pounds, tethered by a yard and a half of chain to a kennel which is no more than a barrel tipped on its side, or a few corrugated iron sheets roughly knocked-up into a draughty hovel. If the owner ever thinks about it at all, he thinks the dog's rough coat is adequate protection from sun and storm. The fact that dogs enjoy comfort as much as we do, never crosses his sluggish mind.

I have talked to a number of men who keep dogs thus and have convinced myself that they are not intrinsically cruel, but simply thoughtless. 'A dog's life' in the hills is traditionally a hard one. Many shepherds genuinely believe that if you don't bring up puppies hard and keep them hard, they won't be able to work hard. So far as the theory about survival of the fittest goes, I suppose they are right. The weaklings soon die off.

Puppies too young to be collared and chained are left to their own devices and, for a while, they are sufficient to themselves. They eat in competition and play at mock battles or 'herding' each other till their energies flag and they go out like a light and sleep it off, before waking to play again. The trouble starts when they come face to face with the poultry.

The first flustered hen, cackling off for home, may send them scurrying for cover too. But the boldest and brightest pups will soon discover that cackling of hens and farmers' wives are no more than empty threats. So pack leaders of real potential will try again. Next time, one pup will give chase in earnest and round-up the flock while another cuts a victim out. If nobody happens to be around to hear the commotion, the drama will proceed to its inevitable climax and the puppies will enjoy an unscheduled feast that wasn't on their menu.

The pups are not to blame. They simply follow their wild ancestors' instinct to chase and hunt and cut-out a victim. The desire has been deliberately fostered by generations of selective breeding. If their owner deals out a good hiding apiece when he returns to find the carnage, they won't even know what the punishment is for. It is as stupid as thrashing a pup in the morning for the pool he left on the carpet the night before. The dog has no means of associating his 'crime' with his punishment, so that the only result of such chastisement is that the brightest dogs are bound to conclude that men have unreliable and treacherous tempers and that whether they receive a pat or a kick depends not on their behaviour, but on their master's mood of the moment. Nothing is calculated to break canine spirits as effectively and the more intelligent the dog, the more likely he is to be cowed.

Only a minority of stockmen are such fools. Many may be hard, both with their dogs and with themselves, for life in the high and lonely hill country, where only sheep can thrive, *is* hard. But he would be a soulless lout who did not appreciate the help and companionship of a good dog. Dramatic skylines, rugged grandeur and the wild music of calling curlews may be a recuperative tonic for a few days' holiday. Tramping the same harsh heather and toe-shattering scree, through blistering heat or blinding snow, in an eternal search for sheep which disappear as mirages over the horizon, would be hell without a dog. It is almost inevitable that deep bonds are formed between the shepherds and dogs who share the same discomforts and are together so much that it is almost as easy for masters to become psychologically fixated on their dogs as the more conventional way round.

Such human–canine mutual admiration evokes a trait in a man as basic and instinctive as his dog's urge to hunt or to be the leader of the pack. Competitive drive, with status symbols as the hard proof of success are not only symptoms of modern society. When a mediaeval shepherd had an outstanding dog, I would lay odds that he didn't hide its light under the tavern bench on Saturday night, or the church pew on Sunday morning. He boasted about it over his ale after the sermon, provoking arguments which could only be settled by rivals taking their dogs out on the hill and testing them against each other in trials of skill and discipline.

Such private contests satisfied most shepherds because their solitary occupation produced independent but introvert minds. If they satisfied themselves that their dogs were best, they were unworried by the opinion of anyone else.

Just as some dogs are born leaders, while others are

submissive, a percentage of shepherds and farmers are as extrovert and status-conscious as industrial tycoons. Their motivation drives them to choose or breed and train outstanding dogs and, far from being satisfied to know that they have a jewel, they never sleep easy till the world knows it too.

Squire R. J. Lloyd-Price, who had an estate in North Wales, appreciated the potential of matching shepherds and their dogs in public, both individually and as international teams. He knew that it would not only be a fascinating spectacle, but that it would also make stockmen even keener and more efficient at their job. So the squire organised the first competitive trial at Rhiewlas, near Lake Bala, on October 9th, 1873. It was instantly popular, attracting ten competitors and three hundred spectators but, although held in Wales, his first trial was won by William Thompson, a Scotsman, running a Scottish-bred dog called Tweed.

He was a small black-and-tan dog, with a white forefoot, a foxy head and a fair coat. It must have been a bit galling for the Welshman who had organised the competition, particularly as his own favourite breed was the Old English Sheep Dog, long on the leg, with bob tail. Unfortunately they have since been largely spoilt by dog show fanatics, who think they look 'quaint.' In common with most other breeds which have fallen into the clutches of commercial exhibitors, they have been ruined for their original purpose by selective breeders, interested in looks alone.

Whatever Squire Lloyd-Price thought about the results of the 1873 Bala trial, the idea latched-on and has been going from strength to strength ever since. Within a couple of years, it was attracting about thirty entries and a couple of thousand spectators, but trials at the original venue were short-lived. In 1878, the Bala trial was merged with trials at Llangollen, where they have been held every year since, except during the two World Wars. Now, there are trials in England and Scotland and Wales, all run under the rules of the International Sheep Dog Society, which was formed in 1906 to govern the affairs of working sheepdogs. As well as controlling conduct and rules for trials, it has kept a stud book of pedigrees of working collies.

The difference between working and show collies is that there is no particular standard of appearance laid down for the dogs that shepherd sheep. Proof of their looks is in their deeds. A great many of such pedigrees can be traced back to the blood of Old Hemp, bred by a Northumberland farmer called Telfer in the mid-1890s. So, not unnaturally, many of Hemp's descendants carry a family likeness. But there is no hard-and-fast type laid down, as there is for the show dogs under Kennel Club rules, and all that matters with working collies is that they should be capable of shepherding sheep. Those that can't are discarded, or sold for pets, because nobody wants to breed from them.

At most trials there are dogs with rough coats and dogs with smooth; lop-eared dogs and prick-eared; dogs with shining brown eyes and often one or two with 'wall' – or blue – eyes; and it is not uncommon to find a dog with odd eyes, one brown and the other blue. The earthy explanation that this is 'because he had two fathers', is simply rural bait to test just how tall are the stories that townees can be persuaded to swallow!

Coat colour is usually predominantly black, with

A remote farm high in the hills

2 The shepherd told me about his life in lonely places

3 Adoring canine eyes watching their master

4 Tick, my inseparable companion

5 The nicest people team up with the wisest dogs

6 Interjecting sequences at competitors' farms

7 Tim Longton farms in the Pennines

8 He keeps his dogs first and foremost for work on the farm

9 Roy jinked away to the right

10 He licked his chops and sneaked a few yards closer

11 My neighbour lambs a thousand ewes

12 Tim showed me his latest litter of puppies

13 The mass of woolly bleating bodies

14 Roy is so conspicuous

15 He would be a soulless lout who didn't appreciate a good dog

white on head, neck, feet and tail tip, but some sport a lot of brown, some are tricolour, while blue merle was once a fashionable colour. Such details matter little because no good working dog can be a bad colour though, other things being equal, the less white the better.

In mediaeval times, specialised dogs were used by drovers to move cattle and sheep from traditional grazing areas to the centres of populations. Vast numbers of animals were taken annually from the Norfolk marshes to Smithfield. Other drovers brought animals from the downs of Wiltshire or the mountains of Wales.

The distances were so great that the animals were often shod with steel shoes to prevent their horny hooves wearing away to the quick on the journey and they had to graze by the roadside on the way.

The drovers also lived off the country, crossing some of their collies with greyhounds to produce 'Smithfield' lurchers to catch rabbits and hares on the way. This was naturally unpopular with the local landowners who knew that to catch a hare, a dog not only has to be fast but also to be capable of changing direction smartly enough to pick the hare up when she jinks.

This is one of the primary functions of a dog's tail. It uses it as a rudder to shift its centre of gravity, changing balance to alter direction. So laws were passed to exempt cattle dogs from tax only if their tails were docked to make catching hare more difficult. They made them cur-tailed – and that is the origin of the word curtail.

Highly specialised dogs are still used in Australia and New Zealand. The drovers, as well as having dogs to catch hares, used dogs to guard and dogs to drive. In New Zealand, they still have 'drivers' which only work behind the flock; 'headers' to keep the leading sheep in check; 'flankers' to prevent straying on either side; 'huntaways' to gather up the stragglers, and 'yard dogs'. Good modern British working sheepdogs are versatile enough to do the lot.

Sadly, these Border collies have now become so popular that their value escalated until commercially minded dog show-ers cast beady eyes at them. Their application for recognition by the Kennel Club was granted in 1976, so that they were able to form a group called the Border Collie Club of Great Britain, with the object of putting working collies on the show bench, to be judged by an arbitrary standard of points for appearance – but not for work.

The Shetland Sheep Dog was once a useful, virile dog but bod show-ers have transformed it, under its dog show name of Sheltie, into an effete pet, only fit for ladies' boudoirs. The Old English Sheep Dog (the bob-tailed dog), favourite of the famous Squire Lloyd-Price who started sheepdog trials, is now 'way-out' enough to appear on TV commercials – but seems to have lost the folk memory of how to work sheep.

Small wonder, then, that the real sheepdog men are revolted at the idea of their breed being prostituted on the show bench lest a similar fate befalls it. There is little that can be done to prevent it because the International Sheep Dog Society does not even specify that 'Border' collies be used in its trials. It was so obsessed with working qualities – rightly so, in my view – that it has always been prepared to register *any* dog that satisfies the officials that it is proficient at working sheep. Collies of other breeds could be registered with the ISDS and, if they were good enough, could win trials. The fact that they don't is a yardstick of just how good the genuine working collies are – and how stupid it will be if their blood is diluted by insistence that competitors have pedigrees dominated by the so-called beauty (!) standards dreamed-up by the people whose only contact with sheep is a pair of woolly underpants.

Whatever the Border Collie Club may do, the signs are that the International Sheep Dog Society will ignore their interfering rivals and continue to run sheepdog trials for the owners of genuine working sheepdogs. They already have a register of working sheepdogs extending to over 90,000 entries in twenty-seven volumes.

Sheepdogs have also made a name in Obedience Trials where handlers match their dogs to perform a stereotyped set of tests better than any of their competitors. They have to walk, as if glued, at their boss's heels, whichever way he turns and whether he walks fast or slow, moves or stops. They have to stay, on command, when he walks on, either sitting or standing or lying down; and they have to remain motionless in the ring, when the boss goes out of sight and leaves them.

Before the first afternoon of such a sport was over, the pleasure would pall for me and leave me rigid with boredom, although I must admit I should find it infinitely preferable to a dog show. For those that like it, the Border collie is so anxious to please that he can outshine almost any other breed. But some trials are run under the auspices of the Kennel Club, and now that the Border Collie Club is affiliated, promising dogs which are not registered may be eliminated. So the whole business of trying to shackle working dogs in dog show fetters seems excessively stupid.

Eric Halsall, who has been so closely involved with sheepdog trials for so many years, is both bitter about it and unprintably articulate! Fortunately, it is always easy to divert him back to his favourite topic and, since he is a nice-natured man, he instinctively remembers the pleasant aspects.

One of the real perils of hill farming is sudden, heavy snowfall. Everyone expects snow in such lonely heights and takes precautions against it. Most farms, in such places, have a few small, stone-walled fields in the in-bye close to the house.

Ideally, the flock is driven here the day before a storm. Then the land doesn't get puddled by sharp hooves for longer than necessary, nor does concentrated dung foul the pasture. As soon as the weather lifts again, the sheep are driven back to fresh pastures. But that is easier said than done. The weatherman on the wireless is notable chiefly for his inaccuracies. He is reasonably good at saying what happened yesterday, but inept at predicting ahead. When there is a patch that is set-fair or set-foul for several days, he notches up correct guestimates by saying it will continue, but is conspicuously shaky at foretelling the change!

Shepherds know better than to stick their necks out except in their own locality. The distant sea showing up sharp as brittle ice could mean nothing nationally, but the first cloud on the horizon may sweep up the valley every time, heralding local storms which are certainties in the betting books of local men.

When we were filming at Tim Longton's, no change in the outlook was obvious to me, nor had the Met. Office forecast one. But Tim shaded his eyes towards Morecambe Bay and told Philip to look sharp with this shot before thunder rain sluiced down the spout of his camera. He was quite right.

Eric laughed when he heard about it, but it reminded him of a sudden snow-storm that had blotted out a complete flock in the border country. The sheep had gone for shelter and several had fallen through a snow drift into a crevice. A shepherd on his own could have slid down to join them in their peril and, even if he had been equipped with radar or sophisticated electronic gear which discovers wrecks on the ocean bed, he wouldn't have found those sheep. Eric's dog treated it as a routine patrol, and within minutes was 'pointing' those missing sheep with the confidence of a Gordon setter which has found a grouse.

'I've never made up my mind *how* he did it,' Eric said, 'because some sheepdogs seem to use their ears as effectively as asdic on a minesweeper, while others have noses as sensitive as blood hounds.'

He told me of dogs which had gone miles to the farmstead for help when their master had slipped and broken a limb in wild places; and one that had almost starved by the corpse rather than desert his beloved boss who had died of a heart attack.

It reminded me of Mick, a mongrel bull terrier, with which I grew up. When I was a kid of eight I had been sent to post some letters, but fell down and split my knee so badly that I couldn't move at all. Several passers-by came over to pick me up, but Mick guarded me so viciously that it was almost an hour before someone had the wit to go and fetch my father!

The more Eric told me about 'his' breed, the more it drove home that it is not specific in-bred qualities so much as basic canine instincts which have brought success. As he recalled feat after triumphant feat, he kept mentioning some magic quality to which he referred as 'eye'. 'This dog had a swine of a ewe that kept breaking away from the bunch,' he said. 'It was only the dog's superlative eye that conquered her.' 'That dog's eye was too strong,' as he described another marathon. 'The shepherd couldn't get him moving again.'

Tim Longton had mentioned 'strong eyes' in relation to early crosses of setters in the breed but watching Tick, my pointer, work, I have often been uncertain when she has 'pointed' at a tussock containing a rabbit or pheasant, whether it was her eye or nose or ears that froze her into immobility. She often stops dead in full gallop with her sensitive nostrils quivering in anticipation. Her nose indicates the general direction of her excitement – but not how far ahead the focus is. Sometimes she stops in her tracks as she comes through the kitchen 'pointing' at the wall or skirting board. In this case, the quarry is usually a mouse and I believe that it is her ears which have alerted her rather than her nose. And often, when I have been sitting motionless in the wood, waiting to see what's about, she will tense-up when she sees – and I see – a movement in the undergrowth, but neither is sure what it is. So I am quite certain in her case that nose or ears or eyes will all trigger-off her intense concentration, but the fact that she 'points' at the spot which interests her is really a sign of her uncertainty rather than that she is being 'strong'. If she can confirm by eye or ear the *precise* spot where her nose has indicated that a rabbit is hiding, she will often take a flying leap and capture it. A fox hunting voles will do exactly the same.

So I asked Eric to tell me more about 'strong eyes'.

'If a dog is bringing a bunch of sheep up to a pen,' he said, 'there is almost always a leader. More often than not, it is an old ewe. There is still enough wild instinct in sheep to instil the same fear of being trapped as any truly wild animal has. So they've always got their eyes skinned for the slightest chance to escape. The nearer they get to the pen, the more urgent it becomes to probe for a weak spot – and some old ewes are very stubborn and strong-willed. If they do decide to make a bolt for it, they take the hell of a lot of stopping.'

I've seen precisely the same drama when Tick is herding pheasants though, in their case, sheer panic rather than tough cunning is the driving force.

Eric went on to explain that both the shepherd and his dog are aware of the psychological urge of sheep not to be caught by the dog or his master. The nearer the sheep gets to what she regards as being trapped, the more keenly she looks for a weak spot through which to make a dash. The dog knows this and the tension builds between them. When the ewe stops, indecisive, the dog stops too and stares her out, absorbed in utter concentration, determined to forestall any break for freedom.

It was the initial cross with setter that imparted the unflinching stare, that eventually subdues the most arrogant sheep, convincing her that escape is impossible because her adversary's concentration will enable him to anticipate the best laid subterfuge.

It is this fascinating battle of wills which makes sheepdog trialling so absorbing. The drama is never played the same way twice because the sheep are forever trying to discover a gap the dog hasn't thought about, always ready to take advantage of the slightest error of judgment by the shepherd in placing the dog,

79

or any lack of will power by the collie. Close-up on television, it is possible to watch the tension mounting as room for manoeuvre dwindles as the sheep approach the shepherd. A dog with a very strong eye may stare out his adversary but, in doing so, become so involved that the shepherd loses touch with him. A dog with a weak eye allows his attention to wander so that the sheep may be able to take advantage of his butterfly mind.

The permutation of possible errors can escalate with a difficult bunch of sheep or an incompetent shepherd. However good a dog trainer and handler may be, no man will manage sheep well until he understands sheep psychology as intimately as he understands the working of his own dog's mind.

Sheep, like people, are often led by the most cunning female in the flock and the shepherd must know enough about his job never to put his dog at a disadvantage by giving a command with less than superb timing. Not only must a dog have a good eye – but so must his master. So it would be far more difficult for an ordinary dog owner to win a sheepdog trial than for a working farmer or shepherd. He couldn't get the practice with sheep for one thing, but however brilliant he is with dogs, it takes years of experience to know enough about sheep to give the right commands at the exact psychological moment. If he isn't steeped in mutton broth enough to make him capable of thinking like a sheep, he'll never be able to see into the sheep's mind quickly enough to forestall it. He must know the off-beat tricks of the trade, that sheep move naturally down hill at dawn but instinctively seek the higher ground as evening falls. A young dog's task can thus be eased or made more difficult, depending on whether he is asked to help sheep do what comes naturally – or prevent them.

It's the really awkward old beggars that tempt a dog to 'grip'. That's shepherd's jargon for catching hold, and it's a crime for which a dog and his master can be disqualified. It's less of a crime at home! Whatever they say about 'following like sheep', you can't follow where there isn't a leader, and many old ewes are both cunning and stubborn. So, if they really are set on mutiny, it is vital to have a dog that will stand his ground and discipline the delinquent – and the only tool he has is a set of powerful teeth. Once the sheep have tasted who is master, they won't try it on again but it takes real skill on the shepherd's part to allow his dog enough scope to assert dominance, but not enough to acquire a taste for raw mutton!

Eric said that dogs that really do get too tough with their sheep are down-graded to cattle dogs. Cows have got a very painful kick that will send a dog spinning for yards, inflicting punishment more severe than the heaviest-handed master would deal out. Having tried that once, the dog has got to have high courage to risk a second helping, so that second-raters may be cowed and refuse to come back for more. A nasty heifer, protecting a new-born calf, can be even more forbidding so that a dog which can gaffer her certainly commands admiration.

Men like Tim Longton who keep both cattle and sheep are not interested in dogs unless they are able and willing to work both. Circus tricks on trial grounds are all very well for weekend entertainment, but their dogs earn most of their living at home.

I have always loved lurchers and, compared to a collie, even the roughest-coated lurcher is pretty lightly clad. It comes of generations selectively bred to run fast enough to catch hares – but a spell of hot weather will crease even the best lurcher in a run of very few minutes.

I discovered this to my cost when Gypsy, the best bitch I ever had, put up a hare in a very large field of new-mown hay on a scorching summer day. Every time the hare got near a hedge, the old bitch ceased pursuit and dashed to cut off her retreat, as a collie would get round a bunch of sheep. When the hare turned for open ground and Gypsy closed-up for a wrench, her quarry always jinked at the last split second and evaded her. The drama developed for two or three minutes during which the old bitch almost succeeded time after time. Then I noticed the hare was gaining ground and that the old bitch was running stiffly – but still trying. The hare made it through a gap in the hedge, followed by the dog, who was not twenty or thirty yards behind. She was a wonderfully game bitch and never gave in while she could see her quarry, so they pounded on across the next great prairie field till the hare disappeared in standing corn. When Gypsy came back, I noticed her front feet were brushing the ground in a bizarre, stilted shuffle. Her eyes were glazed and her tongue lolling out in a caricature of a canine grin. She lifted up her muzzle because experience had taught her I was more effusive in my sympathy or praise than the shepherd's laconic 'That'll do', but she got no pleasure from my congratulation because, by the time I had bent to pat her, she had rolled over rigid and unconscious in a fit.

Dogs can only sweat through tongues and feet so that they find it impossible to get rid of the urea and other waste products of exertion and to lower their temperature by sweating through skin pores as we do.

Exceptional effort, in great heat, will sometimes render them unconscious in a ureamic fit, and I thought for a while that my old bitch would die. As things turned out, she recovered, but it taught me never to allow her to over-exert herself in such blistering weather again.

It was a lesson I never forgot, and seeing sheepdogs working in hot weather always reminds me of it. The specialised fox hounds which are used for the sport of hound-trailing are got so fit they don't carry an ounce of spare fat. They are solid bone and muscle which reduces their necessity to sweat. Even so, they are often shaved with a razor, not to reduce their weight but to keep them cool, and they are given a minimum of liquid before they run.

Working sheepdogs, on the other hand, have coats thick enough to keep out the winter, and they will cover up to a hundred miles a day, up and down mountains in shine as well as storm. Shepherds naturally try to work out of the heat of the day for the sheep's as well as the dogs' sake but even so, I know of no other breed which could work consistently under such conditions.

Anyone who has kept lurchers will know how dangerous it is to take them onto an old airfield which is often a favourite place for hares. Hares have dense pads of fur on their feet, so they often choose to run on the tarmac runways. They get a good grip and can jink and turn effectively. Dogs have smoother, hairless pads which give relatively less adhesion so that they tend to skid. They also have small, clawless 'stopper' pads behind the bottom joint of their forelegs and, when they try to turn suddenly on tarmac or stone, this stopper comes in contact with the ground and is often worn completely and painfully away.

Sheepdogs do not course hares. Not during their working day at any rate! But the loose stone scree, cascading down almost precipitous slopes of wild fell sides, must be terrible stuff to run on and nobody but a fool would allow a running dog, either greyhound or lurcher, anywhere near it.

Eric Halsall was not impressed by the argument. Scree was just one of the hazards of a sheepdog's life. 'There are,' he said, 'over twenty million sheep in the British Isles, in country ranging from wild fellsides to fertile lowland farms. Any canine fool can manage them on the lush pastures, surrounded by fences, but the brainiest inventor has never dreamed-up a gadget to control sheep in wild country half as efficiently as a clever dog. Without dogs, hundreds of thousands of hillside acres would be barren and worthless.' But he didn't deny the life was tough for dog and man.

'The real answer,' he thought, 'lies in brilliant stockmanship. Not only have farmers developed specialised sheep to suit different terrain, but highly specialised dogs to shepherd them. In addition to the qualities of fetching and driving and singling – which are mainly mental – he has bred-in toughness and stamina and hard, cat-like feet, which will stand up to rough stone and scree when most breeds would be limping cripples.'

'What about eyes, then?' I asked. 'Selective breeding didn't do much for sheepdogs' eyes, did it?'

Eric eyed me coldly, making rude sucking noises with his stinking pipe. He played for time and tapped out some goo in the ashtray, refilled it and tamped the next noxious charge into condition to set fire to it. 'The truth is,' he said, 'that for a good many years you would have been right. But you're not now. Some of the early dogs were absolutely brilliant at shepherding, but they did have a tendency to go blind at four or five years old. Progressive retinal atrophy, the complaint is called. There is no such thing as a perfect dog. It's always a matter of compromise. A dog may be fast and keen, but liable to grip. Or a clever dog may be too clever to take risks, and surrender to a stroppy ewe guarding her lambs, instead of gaffering it.

'Well, in the early days, there were some brilliant dogs – marvellous for a few years – but they didn't last very long before going blind. Selective breeding had produced the strong points needed for shepherding but, unfortunately, had, at the same time, "selected" the weakness of eyes prone to deteriorate prematurely. Some people thought that this was an acceptable risk for the certainty of a few years' excellence.' He eyed me through his cloud of smoke to test the effect of the theory.

'I don't consider it an acceptable risk,' I replied. 'I reckon it is as bad as dog show-ers, who have turned bull dogs into pathetic, wheezing monstrosities, with heads too big to be born except by Caesarian operations, or a dachshund with belly so low his penis scrapes the ground. Selective breeding is only sensible so long as the qualities selected are not at the expense of soundness.'

'I'll go with that,' Eric said, 'and so will the International Sheep Dog Society. There is a vet at most big trials who will examine dogs' eyes to see if they are going blind. If they are, they are not bred from and the Society will not register pups of any collie that has failed the test. The snag is,' he went on, 'that you can't be sure until two years old, and a lot of damage may have been done by then. We did try to make testing compulsory, but there are always a minority of money-grabbers who won't agree in case it prevents them selling suspect pups, so it was abandoned again. But the Society has taken steps that are beginning to stamp it out.'

Having seen scores of dogs working superbly at eight or ten years old, I am perfectly happy that the policy has teeth.

"... as a canine projectile..."

Chapter Five

KINDERGARTEN

There are various ways of persuading viewers to tune-
in to the next programme in a series. One of the most
effective is to leave some episode unfinished so that
curiosity is aroused to see what happens next.

One Man and His Dog has a competitive thread
from first to last, so that there is always the incentive
to become involved with a team or man or dog and
be anxious to cheer it on and hope that it will emerge
triumphant in the end. But Philip Gilbert likes more
than one string to his bow so he decided that it would
be interesting to show the development of a collie
from a vandal pup, through training, until he was a
highly competent worker. He decided to revisit the
same farm over the period of training, and film at
various stages. He could then show a sequence, of four
or five minutes, in each programme so that viewers

would switch on next week to see how 'their' pup was coming on. Once switched-on, if the programme was any good, they would stay switched-on to enjoy the whole thing.

Glyn Jones won the Brace Championship in the first series, running Gel and Bracken, a dog and a bitch, together as a team. It was a superb demonstration of mastery of sheep psychology and of partnership between a man with two dogs which seemed equally capable of stealing the thoughts from the back of his mind. Almost before the idea entered his head, it seemed they grasped it by telepathy.

It wasn't as mysterious as it looked. He could make one dog go right and the other left, one start while the other stopped, because he had two entirely separate codes of command. Quite simply, he spoke to one in Welsh, the other in English!

When he had won the championship, I went out to interview him so that viewers could share his triumph – and perhaps, I hoped, his secret. Glyn is no strong silent man of the backwoods. He is slight and wiry, with a wicked sense of fun and the unstoppable volubility of articulate Welshmen.

'Why do you talk Welsh to one and English to the other?' I asked. His expression was inscrutable except for his merry eyes, which always give the game away. 'Gel is my dog,' he said, 'and I am Welsh. So naturally Gel understands his native language. But I married an English girl and Bracken is her dog. Bracken talks English.' But he omitted to explain how he whistled to one in English and the other in Welsh!

One of the greatest pleasures of my job is that it often throws me in contact with chaps like Glyn. Although one of us is Welsh and the other English, we have a common love of dogs and quiet places and tend to laugh at the same things. He was such a 'natural' on television that it wasn't necessary to 'interview' him because we chatted naturally. I was delighted to discover that Philip had asked him to show me exactly how he trained a pup.

The first time we went to film him was early in the year, before the pup had started anything but basic training. I was a bit disconcerted to discover his budding canine star, whose progress we were to monitor, answered the name of Glen. My genius for putting the wrong names to faces gave plenty of scope for confusion between Glyn and Glen.

They live in just the sort of place I would choose for a holiday. High in the Welsh hills, a few miles from Ruthin, the approach in good weather is along a narrow, winding lane, which peters out into a rough track to Glyn's farm and another yet deeper in the hills. In snow, I imagine it is unapproachable.

Philip and Gerry and the camera crew had been staying overnight at a pub in Ruthin, so I left home about five o'clock to join them for breakfast. Gerry had photostated a large-scale ordnance map, ringed the farm we were going to and added foolproof directions 'in case they had finished breakfast and left before I arrived'. She always expects the worst. The directions were supplemented by a precise brief of what Philip hoped to film, with a dossier of background information about Glyn, his dogs, his trial successes and the size of his farm. Such inside knowledge makes all the difference between producing an interesting or a purely superficial interview, but too few producers or assistants bother with such homework.

I'd only met Glyn once before, when he'd won the

Television Trophy Brace Championships. He was in the Welsh International team with Hemp in 1968 to 1970, and with Gel and Bracken in the Brace in 1972, 1973 and 1975. He won the Supreme Championship in 1973 at Bala, and was Reserve at York in 1975. Gel followed up winning the Television Trophy Brace of 1975 by beating Tot Longton's dog (who won in 1976) for the Brace Champion of Champions. A formidable trainer and handler – with two formidable dogs. I'd never met his wife Beryl, who owns Bracken and talks English, but the moment we drove into the yard, we were all asked inside for coffee, biscuits and home-made cakes. The sort of hospitality that genuine countryfolk take for granted, but which distinguishes civilised living from the stupid, competitive urban rush that is replacing it.

Philip shoved his mental shoehorn between us and our comforts as soon as he decently could, and prised us out to get on with the job. He never throws his weight about, but if anyone who works for him can still stand up unaided at the end of the day, he reckons he is slipping!

Not that such a job is work to me because I would rather film Glyn, training a pup like Glen, than have an exotic holiday anywhere else. We left Bracken lying by the cooker in the kitchen, collected Gel who would get things on the rails again, if the young hopeful made a muck of it, and went out to the buildings to meet him.

Spring-Heeled Jack was the name that came to mind. The instant Glyn opened the bothy door a crack, the pup was out, skimming round the yard so fast that he never had all his feet on the ground at the same time. A little flock of poultry, scratching on the muckheap, exploded in a puff of feathers, as the canine projectile disrupted their peace, and Glyn's remark that he was full of the joys of life was an optimistic understatement. He let him whizz round for a few minutes to siphon off his surplus zest, and then called him quietly to heel.

The transformation was dramatic. One second he had been racketting round, apparently out of control, the next he was as tranquil as a staid old dowager. We walked together up the hill above the farmstead to a lovely, sloping field at the head of the valley. There were dramatic rugged mountains as a backcloth, but Glyn's farm was green and spangled with brilliant wild flowers. A lark was singing overhead and dense hawthorn hedges not only promised shelter for stock, but for song birds too.

Philip had been there the evening before and had decided exactly where he wanted Glyn to train his dog so that his camera would catch the effect of exciting lighting. He had chosen a background which would fall away to infinity when sheep and dog disappeared over the horizon. He already knew just where he would site his camera, and how far ahead he wanted Glyn and me to work; how the sequence would start and how, he hoped, it would finish. But, first, he had to establish in viewers' minds where we were, who Glyn was and what he hoped I'd see.

Philip chose a photogenic mossy bank and got the two of us sweating and heaving to shift a tree trunk to where he wanted us to sit, and to camouflage it so that it looked as if it had always been there. It is a poor job that won't stand a foreman, and his qualifications are such that he should never be out of work. When we had scene-shifted – almost mountain-moved! – the trunk to his liking, sitting down on it was about all we were fit to do. Gel was on one side of his master, so I was able to remind old viewers and tell new that here were two of the combination that had won the last Brace Championship. Glen then made his bow as, I hoped, a star of tomorrow who would demonstrate how it was done from the kindergarten, and what a budding champion looked like in the making.

Most people who keep dogs, whether they are enthusiasts like me or simply the owners of family pets, are interested to know more about how to train them. I was delighted at the prospect of watching a trainer of international repute at work.

That first day, it was the basic stuff. 'Come' and 'Sit' and 'Stay', the sort of thing I start a puppy on at ten weeks old and repeat and repeat every time I feed him, till his compliance is a reflex. Glen was seven or eight months old, already good at the basics, but I wondered why Glyn had left him so long before getting him steady to sheep.

He told me much the same as Tim Longton had. He said that sheep were fast and stubborn enough to keep going for a gap, when once they had made up their minds about possible escape. If one collided with a puppy, it would hurt him as much as if he had been given a good hiding. If the pup didn't understand that such punishment was for nothing worse than not keeping out of the way, it might either break his spirit or turn him savage in revenge. So Glyn lets his dogs get a bit of size in them before commencing serious work. Although I can see the point, I have always believed it is far easier to nip bad habits in the bud as they first show up, than it is to cure them after they are formed. So I like to begin training my dogs at a few weeks old.

There is so much hanging about when filming,

even with a producer like Philip, that everyone gets to know everyone else extremely well. Too well, if you don't hit it off. While cameras were being moved and realigned, I discovered that Glyn does not subsist entirely off his farm. He works on different days of the week at two local cattle auctions, marshalling sheep and cattle from transport wagons to selling pens, and after the sale is over, into the cattle trucks of the men who have bought them. Being there regularly, he knows most of the farmers and dealers and butchers personally. His shrewd mind calculates from nods and winks and odd hints dropped, when prices are likely to be best for buying and when for selling.

Although his acreage is not large, by modern standards, his specialist inside knowledge helps him exploit it to the full. The fringe benefit, of course, is for the dogs. Nothing tries and develops a dog's skills better than working with strange sheep and cattle all the time. Sheep on the home farm soon get to know their own dog, how tough he is and exactly how far they can try it on with him. If he is pretty good, the least line of resistance is to comply with his wishes on the principle 'If you can't beat him, join him.'

He would be a modest hound who did not get swollen-headed from such treatment, but there is no such danger for dogs working in a cattle yard. The fact that sheep and cattle are off their own ground, worried and frightened, makes them difficult to deal with. Drovers' dogs in cattle yards work in a hard school and, if they are of the calibre to live with it at all, it makes rare dogs of them.

At lunch time, we all went into the kitchen where Glyn's wife, Beryl, did us proud with a real farmhouse spread. The conversation flickered round all our mutual interests so that, by the end of the meal, we all felt we knew each other very well.

This is not such an illusion as it may appear. Nothing exposes one's weakesses so ruthlessly as a television camera. The slightest fault involves a retake and there is no camouflaging the cause because everybody saw it happen. The producer and his assistant, the cameraman and sound engineer and whoever else is working there not only saw it, but have extra work because of it. To hammer the nail into the coffin, everybody knows that final proof will be furnished when the film is processed.

So, after every retake, there is no disguising the fact that everyone there has seen you, at your worst, with every blemish in 3-D. Since not all fools are in front of the camera, it won't be long before some retakes occur because the cameraman read a wrong exposure, his assistant didn't focus right, or the sound engineer ran out of tape. Even producers have been known to change their minds and producers' assistants have messed-up continuity! Before long, it is clear to all that nobody is infallible. All being in the same boat forges a link of comradeship, which makes the rest of the assignment a delight, however hard the work.

We spent the rest of the afternoon filming Glen's first introduction to working the sheep. Nobody could cast doubts on his keenness for he would have eaten them if he had had the chance. I have seen terriers eye rats with similar lust, and Tick, my pointer, who hates the guts of grey squirrels, launches herself into the attack with just such abandon.

I became completely absorbed by the battle of wills between Glyn and Glen, but the foundation of basic obedience training just – and only just! – stood the test and the sheep escaped unharmed. He did get close enough to scatter them to the winds at one stage, and old Gel came into his own by being sent to collect and regroup them ready for the next affray.

It was one of the occasions when most of the retakes weren't due to either Glyn or me. The line of approach chosen to give the most attractive scenic background happened to coincide, at one point, with a gap in the fence where the sheep knew they might escape. However good a dog driving them up from behind might be, it really needed a brace partner on that flank to forestall an unscheduled departure. An untrained pup did not have the chance of a cat in Hades.

By mid-afternoon, the temperature had soared into the top eighties and it became obvious that even the best sheepdogs were not as immune to heat as I had thought. I noticed that Glen was showing symptoms of the forefoot shuffle that had preceded the collapse of my lurcher Gypsy when she'd coursed a hare in similar weather. His eyes had a faraway expression so that it looked as though he was on his last legs. I mentioned it to Glyn, who had also been worried, so we packed up as soon as possible with the idea of continuing in the cool of the following morning.

Nothing is more boring than propping up the bar in some provincial hotel until it is time to go to bed, so Glyn and Beryl joined us and we all ate out at a pleasant place that only the locals knew about. Glyn and I had been getting the thick end of the stick all day. We were fellow victims – and Beryl was agog to hear all about it. Philip was monarch of all he surveyed when the cameras were rolling and Gerry, although the next rung down the ladder, was still far above us in the television peck order. But all men are equal with a glass in hand and an elbow on the bar, so Glyn and I launched ourselves into a colourful, if highly inaccurate, account of the day's events for Beryl's benefit.

We were no longer puppets dancing to every tweak of a producer's string or nudge from his assistant. According to us, the dog had done marvels – when the camera was pointing the wrong way; and anybody but a city slicker would have known that you can't make an old ewe and a young dog smile like stuffed dummies, through the same camera lens, except in a television commercial. We went into great detail about how Glyn and I had been the down-trodden underdogs, who could have finished the job in half a day – if only we'd been in charge. All but Beryl knew we were spoofing and, since women tend to gang-up, even she believed Gerry in preference to us! It was one of those memorable evenings that makes everybody present friends for life.

By nine o'clock next morning, Philip had got us at it again. This time he hoped to capture on film just how Glyn controlled the pup, when he wanted him to go right or left. The natural instinct, for a dog, is to walk (or run!) towards sheep, and his basic training had slowed him down enough to move at a fairly controlled gait. Since the instinct is to drive his quarry, it is also natural to weave from side to side to keep them in a bunch. So we walked behind the dog and waited until he veered either to right or left. Every time he went right, Glyn said, 'Away to me' and, when he went left, he called 'Come bye'.

It was astonishing how quickly the sheepdog's sharp mind associated his own movement with his master's command, and once the idea had clicked, how quickly he learned to respond. We were wearing radio microphones so that our conversation could be recorded on the sound track of the film without the bother of lugging cables with us. This made it possible to see from the film whether Glyn said 'Come-bye' before or after the dog veered left. When we started, it was crystal clear that he was merely implanting in his pupil's mind the association between deed and word. Gradually, the man's mind asserted his dominance and the dog was so keen to please that he moved, as if controlled by invisible wires, the moment he heard the command.

It was an impressive demonstration of associated ideas growing strong enough to produce an automatic reflex action. From then on, all that was necessary was to repeat the lesson so often that the words 'Come-bye' and 'Away to me', or their whistled equivalents, put the dog in the precise relationship to his quarry that the shepherd wanted.

When he had got Glen going right and left, with confidence, to voice commands, he began to train him to the whistle. He just started him going to the right – and then gave his whistle command for 'Right'. The pup picked it up incredibly quickly and had got the whole range of whistle commands synchronised with the relevant voice commands within a few days. Indeed, it demanded almost as much concentration by Glyn as his dog because each whistle command had to be specially composed for Glen alone so that Glyn could work several dogs at the same time, each responding only to his own coded whistle. If the shepherd is careless and does not arrange whistles distinct enough from those he is using for his other dogs, or even if he picks two names that sound too alike, a young dog will often get confused.

We returned, at intervals, during the summer and

early autumn to monitor further progress, and discovered that one of the hardest things to teach a dog is to drive sheep *away* from his master. It comes naturally to round them up, because it is part of the primitive urge to get round the quarry and demoralise it by making it panic away from the safety of escape towards the waiting pack. It is natural to 'fetch', or drive, them towards the shepherd, who has replaced the dominant pack leader in the eyes of his adoring dog. But a master who requires a successful hunter to drive his prizes *away*, into safe obscurity, would be sent to a canine psychologist if sheepdogs were capable of diagnosis.

Glyn got over the problem by getting behind the sheep with the dog. When man and dog approached, the sheep moved off and the dog's natural instinct was to rush round, to head them, and bring them back to his master. Simply by forcing him to the left, every time he tried to go right, and vice versa, Glyn kept him behind his sheep and his very presence there kept them moving, or being driven away. When things did look like going wrong, a long shrill whistle blast, to stop, clapped him on the ground as if he'd been shot.

The next, and perhaps the most exciting, lesson was to 'shed', the shepherd's term for shed one off, or split it from the rest. The whole process was an exercise in channelling basic instinct into a sophisticated routine.

From Glen's point of view it must have been pure delight. He was sent out and allowed to swing off in a lovely pear-shaped arc to bring him directly behind his sheep, so that they were in a straight line between him and his boss. This is the classical 'gather' that starts every run in every sheepdog trial. When the sheep saw him, they bunched, the leading ewe stamping a petulant forefoot in impotent annoyance before setting out with her bevy directly towards the shepherd.

Glen was wreathed in smiles, triumphant that he was forcing all his quarry to deliver themselves to his beloved master. On they came, directly towards him, till Glyn sensed they would come no nearer willingly, and that the leading ewe had transferred her animosity from the dog to him. He used his deep knowledge of the ways of sheep to drop the dog at the precise distance that made them indecisive whether to worry most about dog or man. They dithered whether to bunch or bolt; and, if the verdict favoured bolting, whether to choose his right side or his left. The result was inevitable and their mental vacillation escalated till the leader lost her domination. Morale slumped, transferring the sheepish jitters into a physical rhythm, rocking them first in this direction and then in that, as weak resolves to bolt were upset by later plans. Before long, the inevitable happened; skilfully prompted by Glyn's pointing crook, half the bunch began to move one way and half the other, leaving a momentary gap in the middle.

'Come here,' said Glyn, calling the dog, and the sudden movement split the sheep into two separate bunches as the dog bounced through.

The dog didn't even know what he'd done. He'd come as called and, in so doing, had 'shed 'half the sheep one way and half the other. Next time, Glyn would only have to wait that little extra time, till a solitary sheep split away from her fellows, before calling the dog through the gap to single it in copybook fashion.

For his part, Glen had enjoyed the exercise as much

as his primitive ancestors or modern wild relations would relish cutting a victim out of the herd. So Glyn's praise was a bonus. A very special bonus, as it happened, because he was so delighted to have demonstrated a perfect first shed to the camera that he couldn't conceal the excitement in his voice. 'That'll do,' he said but, for once, it didn't sound like grudging praise.

The basic training took about four months, by which time the dog would obey commands without hesitation. As his experience broadened so that he understood why he was being asked to go right or left, or to stop or start, it was vital to watch that he didn't develop into a know-it-all who might make wrong forecasts of what his master wanted. For this reason, the very best trials dogs are often aged between five and eight, so that they have time to develop an almost telepathic partnership with their handlers and are still young enough to outmanoeuvre the slyest mountain sheep.

By the time we had made a short, but complete, film of Glen's training, it had become so obvious that Glyn had not put his shirt on a loser that Philip invited him to bring the young dog for a spin round the 'real' course we would be using for the Television Trophy. Nobody expected that such a young dog could, by then, be up to National Trial standards but we thought that viewers, who had enjoyed watching his training, might like to see him try his skill in the same arena as the very top dogs. We all looked forward to meeting the whole family again then.

Nothing worthwhile is easy, so I knew that the improvements we had seen in the pup over the few weeks between our visits were not produced by luck. Glyn confided that, 'Between now and then, I'll give him all the work I can on the farm.'

Philip had already decided that 'A Sheep Dog's Year' would be an attractive item to include in the next series. Not as a single wodge but as a regular spot of four or five minutes in each programme, as he did with Glyn Jones' training of his pup. Both would have the effect of breaking-down otherwise long periods of pure competition. Both would involve viewers with the feeling that they were watching 'their' dog's progress in training or sharing his triumphs and disasters in all weathers on the hill.

Lambing is no time for a young dog to start work. The ceaseless battle for the lives of ewes and lambs would wear the most saintly patience thin and shepherds have earthy souls, and work at such pressure that they sometimes lose their cool. Quite apart from the risk of a sharp backhander from a tetchy boss, the chance of punishment from irate ewes is even greater. The most placid old sheep the day before she lambs, can be hell let loose a few hours later, if she thinks her young is threatened. She stamps the ground, to give fair warning, lowers her head and dives to the attack with the agility of a professional pugilist. Old and seasoned dogs take such adversaries seriously. Painful experience has taught them to be one step ahead of the attack, and it is one of the few times they are allowed to discipline their charges by gripping viciously. An unwary puppy, under such circumstances, can find himself spattered against the sheep yard wall before he knows what's hit him.

At such a time, a bold dog is also invaluable as an incentive to a ewe to foster a strange lamb. It is obvious that, when a ewe has licked a lamb dry from the fluid in the embryonic sac in which she carried it, the lamb smells strongly of *her* smell. That is the initial recognition symbol. Soon after that, they learn the sound of each other's voices, but it is only when her milk has passed right through the lamb that she becomes thoroughly fixated. Few ewes will rear more than two lambs successfully, so odd lambs of triplets and orphan lambs when mothers die, are fostered onto ewes who have lost their lambs or are suckling only one.

The traditional way of persuading a ewe to take to a strange lamb is to skin her own dead lamb and tie the skin onto the stranger. 'Her' own smell then fools her that she is suckling her own flesh. If she has produced only one live lamb, there won't be a dead skin to play with, so a good dog is put to cast his 'strong eye' over her and monopolise her attention while the fostered lamb is placed beside her own lamb to suck. This fires her maternal passions so that she becomes overwhelmed by her instinct to protect her offspring and can often be persuaded to take to it without even noticing that it is not hers.

When the lambs are strong enough, they and their mothers are taken up to the hill from the farmstead. Early in the year the grazing is more forward on the lower slopes so that, by morning, most of the flock will have sneaked back as low down as possible, over-grazing the best bits and leaving the rest untouched. Dogging them back is ideal work for youngsters. It has to be done slowly and gently and it gets puppies used to the fact that dashing sheep about separates the ewes from lambs and runs off the profit with worry and unnecessary exertion.

Early summer is shearing time and, in most of the country, the practice is for neighbours to club together in a gang, fetching all the sheep down from the hill, separating them into individual ownerships, helping each other with shearing, and returning the shearlings to their grazing.

They always try to start by about four in the morning. It is cool to work then, and the job is half-done for them because sheep come down naturally at dawn and need less bossing by the dogs. If they were left to mid-day, half of them would be lying-up, away from heat and flies, under dense bracken or in shady nooks, so that even the best dogs would have a job to find them.

When shearing is done, lambs may not even recognise their own mothers. They are moved to the in-bye paddocks round the house, and spend the night bleating out their anguish. Hunger and instinct and a little luck will have united most by dawn, but a steady sensible dog can stir them round gently enough to 'introduce' the few that haven't met, before returning them to the hill.

By the time the flock is brought in again for dipping in August (to kill the parasites) it will usually be time to wean the lambs. They go almost berserk to get back to their mothers which are driven away from them up the hill, so that keeping a whole flock of youngsters under control will soon take the fizz out of the most headstrong pup.

After that, the work is routine for several months. Sheep have to be regularly looked at and counted, moved onto fresh pasture and selected, when ready, for market.

All this will mature the pup, make him ready for testing winter days of low cloud and fog, torrential rain and sudden snowstorms, when it is common for dogs to rescue stranded sheep and it is far from rare for them to help their masters. It is a wonderful time for men and dogs to spend countless hours in each other's company so that their individualities merge and blend and weld into a partnership that is far closer than is common amongst mere men. It is a partnership that can last for eight or ten years before the dog gets too old or stiff for active service. At that stage, some shepherds, who regard their dogs merely as tools of their trade, destroy them as they would scrap a redundant implement. But in most farmhouses tucked away in the solitudes of the hills, the favourite dog is pensioned-off to curl in a corner by the fire and dream of triumphs past and of long hours spent in quiet places with his master.

"... so that cable could be laid..."

Chapter Six

TECHNICALLY SPEAKING

Half an hour's programme on the box seems nothing much. If you don't like it, you can switch it off. If you do like it, it is over all too soon. Seven such programmes seem little more, but the cost of producing them is prodigious. The BBC does not sanction such expenditure lightly, so a detailed market research exercise was carried out on the first series, before the next was sanctioned.

The figures were encouraging because not only did an exceptionally high number of viewers watch it, but a high percentage of those who did, enjoyed it more than average. The impressions were confirmed by a huge postbag from viewers, who might be surprised to discover how much notice the planners take of what they say they like. So those too idle to write, deserve to get the programmes that they don't enjoy!

Although the sheepdog trials were filmed in September, Philip and Eric had started work on them by February. We have recorded one series at Buttermere, one at Loweswater nearby, and another in the York-shire Dales, at Austwick, but the problems at each proved very similar.

Buttermere was chosen for the first series for several reasons. There was a large flat field of lovely grass, spattered with wild flowers. The waters of the lake lapped right up to the turf at one end of the field, while the other boundaries were dry stone walls, composed of random rocks piled higgledy-piggledy. When the sun was going down, the horizontal rays stabbed through the grey chinks of mossy stone so that I had never seen such permanence balanced so precariously.

Towering above this natural arena were purple hills, etched into casual compartments by a whole network of walls, spiders'-webbing away to the horizon. Streams and rills and waterfalls were the veins that fed fertility to the scattered green patches, where sweet herbage tempted little bands of sheep. Their owners lived in the grey stone farmsteads, nestling wherever they could find a foothold that gave them shelter under the brow of a hill, or protected by one of the hanging woods their forefathers had planted.

It was an idyllic spot and it needed no visionary eye to discover why Philip had picked it. The trials could all take place on the arena and the camera could shoot them with a background of lake or, from the other end, against the seductive curves of a pair of fertile mountains. With a flick of his wrist, he could change the scene to angry, tumbling, vicious scree or the prosperity of trim farmsteads, where they were harvesting hay, on the other side of the valley. For close-up shots and interviews, he had the choice of the banks of rocky streams, with snow white Ayles-bury ducks paddling in the shallows; or a farmyard,

106

where the master of the midden was a flamboyant game cock, straight from the frame of an old sporting print.

Such perfection does not come ready-wrapped without a snag or two lurking at the bottom of the package. The land at the other end of the arena, by the lake, was rather peaty and boggy. One of the vital bits of equipment for filming the trial was a Simon Truck weighing several tons. This is a heavy lorry with a huge pair of hydraulic arms, like giant calipers, mounted on the chassis. The bottom of one arm is anchored so that the end of the other arm can accommodate a small platform, big enough to hold a television cameraman with his camera. When the hydraulic calipers are straightened, the platform is raised aloft so that the camera gets a bird's-eye view of the whole arena. Similar contraptions are used in cities and along motorways to lift up the mechanics who service overhead lighting.

This Simon Truck was vital so that one camera could make a continuous record of everything happening below. It was to be kept running continuously throughout each trial, so that the pictures it obtained were always available to 'cover' the gap if anything else went wrong, or to show the scale of the whole operation.

So Philip and Geoff Lomas, the Engineering Manager, went over the ground where they wanted to site the Simon Truck, with a toothcomb, to check that it was sound. The one disaster they dared not risk was getting it bogged down on the way to its initial position – or anywhere they wanted to place it subsequently. As things turned out, the weather was fine and it functioned perfectly, producing superb tele-recording of everything he wanted. Then there was a terrific storm on the day of the finals – and it got bogged down on the way out!

The other vital bit of gear to which the least damage would have been catastrophic was the mobile control room or scanner. This is an enormous van, weighing fifteen tons and containing all the sophisticated electronic equipment to feed simultaneous pictures from six separate television cameras on to screens in a row above the producer. One camera was to be perched half-way up the mountain, about half a mile away, to give a picture of the whole arena, from judges' tent and shepherd at one end, to the pens the sheep were to be released from at the other. It would cover shepherd, dog and sheep and all the obstacles he had to drive them through. One was mounted on the hydraulic platform of the Simon Truck so that it could command a bird's-eye view of the whole trials fields and to give quite a different angle from the camera up the mountain. Two other cameras were mounted on fixed tripods at various vantage points around the field to give close-ups of interesting and dramatic spots. One was on a wheeled camera dolly while a sixth, hand-held, camera could be sent wherever it was wanted on a Land-Rover.

All the pictures from this electronic armament were to be fed back to the scanner, where Philip could view them simultaneously, record whichever he chose, while he gave instructions to each of the cameramen what he wanted him to do next. So the smallest damage to the scanner would prove disastrous.

Fortunately, the ground at the entrance to the field was sound and solid. It would stand up to the load all right. So would the approach road to the farm and the lanes back to the nearest classified road. There was just one snag which occurred in the lane about half a mile from the farm, that sowed ugly seeds of doubt.

It was a very sharp bump, about two feet high and ten feet long – the sort of rise over a hump-back bridge. It posed no difficulties for cars, tractors or any normal vehicle with a short wheelbase – which simply drove up one side, over the bump and down the other – but the scanner was almost thirty-five feet long! The burning question was, would the front wheels of the scanner go over the bump and leave the belly stranded on unyielding rock? The more they measured it, the tighter the clearance seemed until the final conclusion was that it either just would clear the bump – or it just wouldn't! The risk was too great to leave to the last moment, so the engineers mocked-up a dummy chassis with precisely the same length between wheels and the same ground clearance as the real scanner. They towed it onto site to check one way or the other while there was still time to change locations. There was less than two inches' clearance so, if that bump had been a hen's egg higher, we couldn't have run the first series where we did.

Obviously it would be pointless to have a control room capable of channelling pictures from six cameras simultaneously without the cameras to feed back the pictures. So an enormous camera van was stuffed with goodies, ranging from cameras, spare lenses, camera mountings, microphones, waterproof gear for cameramen, umbrellas big enough for any-thing from a fishing contest to a golf tournament, camera tools, camera spares, and the whole magic box of tricks.

That lot would be useless without something to connect cameras half-way up a mountain, on top of a Simon Truck or scattered over the course to the nerve centre in the scanner where Philip and Gerry wielded their magic wands. So a couple of ten-ton cable tenders carried enough heavy-duty cable to feed pictures from cameras to scanner, and from scanner to monitor sets at strategic points around the course. There was one in the judges' tent, so that they could relate what they could see to the story Philip was telling, and another in the competitors' tent so that they and their families could get a few glimpses of what goes on behind the scenes to make such programmes possible.

These monitors looked similar to ordinary television sets and the one that mattered to Eric and me showed the exact picture viewers would see so that we could shape our commentary accordingly when we went to the studio later to put commentary on the finalised programmes. Otherwise, we could easily have described what we had seen from where we stood, which was often quite different from the view through the camera Philip was using at that moment which was what viewers would see. For example, Philip could have been filming a dog and sheep in close-up through telephoto lenses, which was too far away for us to see with the naked eye.

He couldn't show anything, of course, if the cable had not been laid to the right spots – and laying cable and siting cameras normally accounts for some of the biggest delays in a frustrating craft.

Geoff Lomas coped with this by having a special Land-Rover equipped with gear for mounting cable drums, so that cable could be laid and rewound quickly by driving the Land-Rover to the point where the camera was to be connected. This communication cable, as thick as a hosepipe, snaked around the periphery of the trials field from cameras to scanner, and a smaller cable came back to the monitors which gave us the picture viewers would see, so that the whole thing appeared as involved as an insoluble 'cat's cradle'.

Having misspent part of my life as a Time Study engineer in a factory, Geoff's slick, labour-saving cable-laying methods appealed to my sense of economy! As no doubt it did to the riggers because there are few filthier, more uncomfortable jobs than laying and recovering heavy-duty cable over wet and muddy fields.

Such sophisticated gadgetry was vital to allow Philip to maintain a continuous variety of background and scenery, to avoid long sequences of the trials course itself.

So far as possible, Philip covered the actual trials before and after lunch so that we could interview winners and fill-in what commentary was necessary at 'leisure' at the end of the day. Although these interjections would be slotted into their correct places in the programme when it was finally edited, they were often shot under quite different lighting conditions, either because the light was fading or the weather had changed.

So a lighting engineer, complete with all his abracadabra, was laid on to set his arc lights glaring in our faces as we spoke. It caused a lot of banter between Geoff Lomas and me because I always claimed his lights made my nose look as blue as a boozer's. He claimed my nose *is* as blue as a boozer's and it is no part of his job to conceal the fact! As Eric's didn't look so bad, he said it proved his point. Philip put us both in our places by saying he only requested artificial lighting when the daylight was dim enough to make the whole scene look dull and miserable without it. But at least I can have the last word when recalling it in print. It *did* make my nose look blue!

There were two video tape recording machines, one of which recorded the whole sequence from the camera on the Simon Truck. If any camera was in close-up when something dramatic happened just out of its field of vision, it could be recorded, if only distantly, by the camera on high on the Simon Truck, Or, though he never admits it, Philip could camouflage his own lapses – if he made one – by cutting to the master shot from the Simon Truck to fill in any gaps in continuity!

The other video tape recorder recorded the precise views that Philip selected from his nerve centre in the scanner. Such sophisticated electronic gear guzzles up the power; this was supplied by two generators, one of which was a very large, silent machine driven by a diesel engine.

While we were on location filming in the Lake District or Yorkshire, we sometimes recorded two half-hour programmes in a day. On other days, time had to be spent re-laying the course, to give other background shots, so that only one half-hour programme could be recorded. Had we been using conventional film, it could easily have taken several days (apart from editing after it was developed) to do one programme. A considerable amount of script, running order and other paperwork was required. A caravan was needed for an office. This was also used by Andy Bloomfield, the graphics man.

If the programmes had been filmed rather than shot on video tape, there would have been plenty of time, at the editing stage, to dream-up all the captions that were wanted. As it was, each programme was virtually as complete as it would have been if it had been transmitted 'live', so it was necessary to punch the result up on the screen virtually as it happened. So a field telephone was laid from the judges' tent on the course to Andy Bloomfield who assembled his legend, giving the name of the winner, his dog and the marks scored, while the shepherd was still by the pen with the sheep. The result was recorded simultaneously with the winner's interview.

Another signal service Andy did was to provide artist's impressions of the course itself. The sheep were liberated three or four hundred yards from the judges so that, to get the whole scene covered, a camera would need to have been so far away that the scale of the picture would have made it meaningless. So Andy drew the course, with all its obstacles, and traced the path of dogs and sheep with animated arrows that synchronised with Eric's description of the course before the trial started.

When he wasn't doing that, he was amusing himself by doing cartoons of the more embarrassing moments of everyone in sight. And these lightning thumbnail sketches were produced in the hotel bar at night to make a pleasant evening pleasanter!

In addition to the field telephone, the GPO had laid on a post office line to the site by doing a temporary conversion to turn the local farmer's telephone into a party line. The pressure under which some of the top camera crews work would make most people cringe. One told me that he was just completing his twenty-eighth consecutive day, either at work or on the road between jobs, without geting home at all. He regarded it as a yardstick of his skill that demand for him was such, and his high earnings were certainly justified by his results. To such men a telephone is a necessity because hotel bookings for jobs ahead and the complicated domestic arrangements a nomadic life involves can only be made during odd breaks from behind the camera lens.

The total crew involved for the whole operation was about forty. There was the producer and his assistant, and the girl who did the typing and answered the telephone. Her party trick was to insert a spot of dye under her contact lenses so that it was anybody's guess what exotic colour her eyes would be by dinner time at night. There was an engineering manager, six cameramen, five vision engineers and a supervisor in the scanner, four sound engineers including a supervisor, eight rigger-drivers, three video tape recording engineers and an editor, two electricians, two stage managers, a graphics man, a security man to guard the equipment and lastly, Eric and me. About a dozen camped on site or lived in caravans, while the rest migrated to hotels up to twenty miles away when day was done.

It was vital to feed everyone on site during the day time because there was so much capital equipment involved that it would have been uneconomic to keep it idle by breaking for more than an hour for lunch.

George Hutton came to the rescue. He was the farmer who supplied the sheep, hurdles, course fittings and, having a caravan site on his own farm, he was also used to catering. So he and his family provided tea and coffee, sandwiches and cakes, and biscuits and pop in a handy little tent on the edge of the course. It was not only patronised by us, but also by competitors, their families, friends and camp followers.

The one remaining necessity was a loo. Counting competitors, fifty or sixty people were on site for a

114

week so that the primitive wood or canvas-sided cabins that serve the purpose at point-to-points and other country functions, would have been uncomfortably inadequate. So Philip hired an elegant affair, which at least raised us above the grotty standard of the average travelling circus encampment.

A smaller crew could have covered the sheepdog trial on film, but it would have taken longer and could not have done the job as well, partly because it would have been impossible to capture the spontaneity, unless six cameras had recorded simultaneously, as the electronic ones do, in which case the film processing and editing would be utterly uneconomic. The normal procedure of setting up the camera, filming action – and then trying to repeat the whole thing from another angle for editing – is so slow and cumbersome that it is extremely difficult to get a natural result. When endless retakes have been imposed, frustrations are inevitable. The only compensation is that the film cameras are self-contained and lighter, not needing cable nor a scanner.

Video tape is very different. It is like very high quality sound tape, about two inches wide, and a picture can be recorded on it electronically of the type and quality of output from a 'live' television camera. Apart from this higher quality, one of the main advantages is that the result can be viewed the instant the picture is taken instead of having to wait for film to be processed and developed.

The inside of the scanner is as chock-full of gadgetry as the nerve centre of a battleship, the vital section being a row of screens similar to ordinary TV sets, directly in front of the boss-man directing the operation. Above is a single, larger screen, showing whichever picture the director selects. He can swap this for any one of the others simply by pressing a switch, and it is this master image which is transmitted live, if the programme is live, or recorded on video tape for programmes like *One Man and His Dog*.

With film, you have got a complete shot, permanently and from two angles, so that mistakes can be retrieved by editing-in alternative film. It is a slower, gentler approach and film crews are not in the habit of being hustled. This can be infuriating in the field where I work, because animals cannot be persuaded to time their actions to suit the whims of a television film crew, nor is it possible to forecast precisely when the moments of highest drama will occur. So the director makes up his own mind what it is he wants to show, and has time to go mentally broody to hatch up his plot. He would take a section of film, concentrating on the dog's part, and another showing the sheep's reactions.

The final film would tell a composite, creative story as it unfolded in the director's mind. But it would be a story in the fictitious time of how long it was filmed, as opposed to the real time of how long it took. So much happens simultaneously in a sheepdog trial. Sheep are forever looking for ways of escape, dogs get flustered, they exhibit restrained savagery or almost maternal solicitude. Shepherds' expressions flicker from despair to hope with every permutation from panic to confidence.

All these things can be seen simultaneously on the row of screens inside the scanner and the director can punch them up onto the master screen in whatever order and for whatever duration he chooses. They will then be recorded permanently so that the story he tells will have urgent immediacy and infinite variety, from close-ups of a dog's fangs or his master's desperation, to the triumphant partnership once the sheep are resting safely in the pen. The director has told his story factually and eloquently with his pictures rather than his pen – but it needs a very specialised mentality.

Philip Gilbert says that most people working with electronic television live on their nerves and adrenalin. 'It conditions them,' he says 'into making quick decisions, into anticipating what's going to happen, so that you develop a kind of instinct for knowing, without really thinking why, when you're actually going to cut to a particular shot, and at which precise moment you go to the next one. You see a close-up of a dog,' he continues, 'just as it is getting control. So you have *got* to see what the sheep are actually doing. You need a more general shot to confirm what they are doing together, and what emotions flick across the shepherd's face. It would all be meaningless in close-up, so it is vital to relate it to the whole trials course and what its context is in relation to the obstacles – and, throughout, you have to maintain genuine continuity. With film shot at different times, there might be a temptation to over-dramatise by showing only selected – and possibly biased – excerpts.'

With the row of screens from the electronic cameras, the choice is there continuously but that is the simplest part. The other five screens show what the cameras see that is not being recorded at the precise moment, so it is often possible to anticipate a crisis and direct the camera to focus closer-in or widen the angle in time to capture the drama as it unfolds.

Many of the chaps with whom I work on film would flounder in such high pressure and lose control. Working with film, they need a week's notice to make up their minds whether they want tea or coffee. The video tape tycoons, having installed computers in the backs of their heads, take in the whole scene at a glance, record only the shots they want and finish up at the end of the day with an edited version almost ready for transmission. But those quick decisions are enshrined, for better or for worse; they are in the past as much as yesterday and it is useless sighing for what might have been. It certainly sorts out the men from the boys.

Having gone-on a bit about the veracity of video tape, I am bound to confess that all of it is not necessarily used. The time taken for a dog to guide his sheep all round the trial course is pretty variable. A good dog might be quicker than a bad one – though at least one, not up to top dog class, got his sheep going so fast it resembled hare coursing and would have been over in next to no time if they hadn't dispersed in the car park! Difficult sheep can take the best dogs a long time and varying weather conditions also affect them.

Programme planners, on the other hand, are precise in their time allocations, and are apt to chop off anyone in the middle of saying 'Goodbye' if the programme overruns. So most of the competitions were shot silently, except for the shepherd's radio mike, to record the commands he gave to his dog and the general background atmosphere. It gave Philip leeway to remove the least interesting part of the run, to bring it within its alloted span, without cutting anything decisive for the final result. Eric and I then went to the studio at Shepherd's Bush – ironically named – to dub a commentary onto the final version tailored to fit planners' plans.

118

This was the first time that we saw the result of our Lakeland labours, and it is always a thrill to see what has come out when the pudding's been stirred. The interviews and training sequences and film on competitors' farms were all finished so that all we had to do was to put commentary over about twelve silent minutes for each programme. 'All' we had to do!

It is not too difficult to make relatively sensible remarks about a live dog taking live sheep round a trials course in front of one's nose. When all goes well, it is easy enough to predict how long they will take to get to the next critical point, and to frame one's words accordingly.

But imagine a dog driving sheep the whole width of a large field which would normally take two minutes. If it happens to be an uneventful, cross-drive – and the total time for the trial was a minute more than there was space for – Philip will chop the drive part-way, insert a cut-away shot of the shepherd giving an order, and cut back into the drive a minute later. The cut-away shot will disguise the fact that dog and sheep have leap-frogged a minute ahead of themselves – and whoever is giving the commentary will find himself still talking when the relevant action has finished! To get over this without using the expensive facilities of a viewing theatre, Philip uses a portable machine, with a built-in screen on which he plays back a video tape in his office. Eric and I can then sit down in comfort and play and replay it until we know, in advance, exactly what will happen and, only when we have thoroughly digested it, do we go down to the dubbing theatre to see the real thing.

We sit down in front of the screen, transporting our minds from the windowless, foetid studio to the windswept hills where men and dogs were congregated. Watching the action again, with good dogs and stupid sheep, Eric unfolds the drama as it happened, and his words are recorded on the tape as if they were spoken when the action was recorded.

16 A good modern British working dog is always versatile and fit

17 A nasty heifer can be very forbidding

18 Cooling off in the stream after working in hot weather

19 Drovers' dogs in cattle yards work in a hard school

20 Clapped him on the ground as if he'd been shot

21 Fetching the sheep down from the hill

22 The one remaining necessity was a loo

26 The start of a hound trail

27 All that now remains is to get them in the pen

28 Stuck halfway up a mountain

Chapter Seven

MIXED BAG

I have been so involved with dogs since I was eight that I feel half-dressed without one. Mick, my mongrel bull terrier, took the place of brothers and sisters from when I was a child till I went to university. He was the introduction to the keepers and poachers who initiated me to the sporting – and unsporting! – sides of rural life. My first week's wage amounted to forty-five shillings, as compensation for forty-eight hours spent at a factory workbench. I blued the lot on Mick's successor, Grip. He was a Stafford bull terrier, bred of fighting stock, and he was so good at catching rats that we were welcome to wander on any farm for miles around. With Grip as my companion, I served a practical apprenticeship, which breaks down the barriers with almost any countryman I meet.

Dogs like Mick and Grip which were my first love also introduced me to broadcasting, which is my second. So taking part in *One Man and His Dog* suited me to perfection. With the possible exception of the moments of terror-stricken crisis, I know of nothing I enjoy more than working on radio or in television.

When I had no idea how to begin, Brian Vesey-Fitzgerald, a friend whose advice I respected deeply, heaped good advice on me. 'You don't need to have influential friends,' he said. 'All that is necessary is to know *something* that other folk don't know. Plenty of producers will then give you a spin, to see if listeners or viewers enjoy it too.'

He was quite right, of course. Television is a tough profession and I soon discovered that keeper and poacher friends had furnished me with practical, personal experience of things my competitors had only read or heard about. It has kept me in business ever since.

My first appearance on the box was twenty-five years ago with a badger I had hand-reared. John Vernon, the producer, asked me 'what it would do,' and, tongue in cheek, I told him it 'would follow me like a dog'. I omitted to explain that this was not because I had trained it but simply because I would be the only familiar object in a strange world of the studio and that badgers are simply terrified of being lost. The programme was rehearsed so often that the badger learned his way to where his sleeping box was stored and, since he rightly concluded it was a safer refuge than being held in my arms, he bit me at the final rehearsal and retreated to his box. I was extremely lucky that he consented to do his stuff when we went 'live' on the air, half an hour or so later!

It taught me the first of many lessons that wild animals are unpredictable in such strange surroundings and that the odds on something going wrong, even on apparently simple programmes, are uncomfortably high.

With dogs, it depends more on the man than his dog. I have seen the first dither in the mind of a shepherd contaminating his dog by nothing more tangible than pure transference of thought. If the man is aware of an error of judgment, the morale of his dog may also slump into inadequacy. Just occasionally, an exceptional dog will be the better half of a partnership, which helps lame masters over the stiles.

My pointer Tick is such a one. Jess and I collected her seven years ago, on a sweltering summer's day, from a man who lived in an old railway carriage by the river near Bewdley in Worcestershire. He had a practical sense of values. When he came out of the army, he had invested his gratuity in a credit drapery round and, by living without ostentation or extravagance, he had discovered that his working week need be no longer than the few hours it took to collect his debts on Fridays. The other six days of the week he spent with the dogs that shared his home, walking in the woods around at all hours of the day and night, ekeing out his larder with the fish and rabbits and game that came his way, with or without the owners' permission. He equated his profits with his basic needs and did not waste time making surplus wealth to featherbed the taxman.

It was a pretty fair bet that his dogs would be capable of earning their keep since he was not the sort to subsidise incompetents, and so it has turned out. Tick is bold and fearless, a marvellous house dog and always willing to please. Provided I am articulate enough to translate my wishes into commands she can comprehend, it is her pleasure to obey.

Like everything else that lives with us, she has to earn her keep so, at six months old, I convinced George Inger, who was producing *Animal Magic*, that an autumn walk with Tick might make compulsive viewing.

Pointers point instinctively, even earlier than sheepdog puppies try to round each other up. By the time she was ten weeks old, I had trained her to come when I called her, and to sit and walk at heel. Every time I fed her, which was then four times a day, I put her through her whole curriculum. She positively danced for joy at the prospect of demonstrating that she understood each command I gave – and at the certainty of a reward when she had earned approval. But I had no need to teach her to point, for she did so automatically.

When George Inger came up, we visited a friend of mine who was head keeper on a great estate. He had reared eight or ten thousand pheasants and had distributed them in the little woods and spinneys and coverts that were spattered all about the farmland. Some of the tamer poults were still hanging round the keeper's cottage, scrounging an easy living while it lasted. So George lined-up his camera and we filmed part of the gamekeeper's day, as we had filmed Tim Longton on the wild skyline of the hills above Morecambe Bay. Then Tick and I set off to walk by ourselves through the lush prosperity of fertile wooded farmland. 'By ourselves' is not precisely true. There was George and his assistant, a cameraman and his, and a sound engineer loaded like a packhorse with all his paraphernalia. Each sequence was chewed over and discussed so the most photogenic shots were arranged for Tick and me to use as backgrounds for our story. We wandered along lakesides with gaudy waterfowl providing refractory ripples to mesmerise the viewers' eyes. We went in the park, near to a herd of deer, flicking ears and tails at pesky flies, and through a bunch of Shetland ponies which gathered round to gape, as if they'd never seen a man and dog before.

Tick behaved impeccably throughout. She walked at heel, or worked a few yards ahead, according to my wishes. She was steady with stock and intensely interested in all she saw.

But naturally I wanted to demonstrate to all the world precisely how pointers point. Ken Cook, the keeper, kept his pheasants in the areas from which he wanted to drive them for shooting, by scattering corn there an hour or so before it was time for them to go to roost. So, in late afternoon, the rides through the wood were densely peppered with feeding pheasants.

We picked a lovely rising ride, curving away to the western skyline. In a rough patch at the bottom, there was an old cart, left lying where it had last been used, with beautifully spoked wheels rising above an eider-down of wild flowers.

George sited his camera behind the wagon wheel so that the ancient spokes framed a view that melted away towards the setting sun. He sent Tick and me on a long detour, so that we appeared on the skyline, looking down the ride towards the-camera, across the flock of feeding pheasants with the light over our shoulders. Then he gave us the signal to walk towards him.

The dog had never seen so many pheasants – and nor had I. They spread out before us as thick and oblivious of our approach as a flock of barnyard hens. Tick kept at heel but, out of the corner of my eye, I could see her tensed-up and quivering. Most revealing of all, her tongue popped in and out, as rapidly as the forket of a viper, licking her chops in frustrated expectation. I hissed, quietly, 'Heel-up', just to remind her I was watching too, but her manners would not have disgraced a dowager duchess. She shot me such a glare, for implying that she needed any reminder to behave, that I would have dropped dead if looks could kill.

When the first pheasant noticed my approaching figure, he skulked into the bushes and, since panic is infectious, his fellows followed him. One second the ride had been heaving with pecking forms, the next it was empty except for Tick and me. I let her continue, steadily at heel, till we were about fifteen yards from the camera, hidden behind the wagon wheel. Then I whispered 'Try-on' and she slid a few yards ahead, crouching slightly as her sensitive nostrils inhaled the gamey scent of pheasant. There had been so many of them that it seemed impossible to locate the hiding place of a single individual but, sure enough, she came to her point exactly where the camera could watch her best.

I know no birds more stupid than pheasants. They suffer from the delusion that their good looks will get them by, and instead of legging it for safety when danger approaches, they go no further than the nearest bush or thicket, kidding themselves that it will all turn out right in the end.

This one was lucky. We didn't plan to shoot him with anything more lethal than a camera. I crept up behind Tick and, looking down, I could see his gorgeous colours merging miraculously with a patch of autumn-tinted bracken. Tick stood statuesque, glaring at him from a yard away, with as strong an eye as any sheepdog's. Willing him to submission, she

126

had him so hypnotised that he seemed confused as to whether his secret had been discovered or whether his enemy had stopped there by chance and would not penetrate his camouflage – provided he stayed motionless. George had time to move the camera up and get close-up shots, taken over the bitch's head, to prove to the cynical that the portrait of a pheasant really was the same one at which the dog had stopped to point.

Having got what he wanted, the camera was re-sited behind the wagon wheel and I was told to give the signal to flush the bird. 'Get to him' I said, 'put him out' and as she pounced into the thicket the pheasant rocketed into the air and disappeared, in silhouette, against the setting sun. It was a lovely photogenic climax to round off a walk through the parkland scenery of a great estate. And it was the first of twenty-odd appearances that Tick has so far made. She will never owe me a dog biscuit nor a pound of prime steak, however long she lives.

Sadly, such dogs enjoy too short a span. She is now over seven, and Mandy our old lurcher died at fourteen last year, followed shortly after by another lurcher, Spider. So I reckoned it was time to get another pup to take over the hard work when Tick is ready for retirement.

Some years ago, I had a grand alsatian which came to a sticky end when she picked up a dose of strychnine that I believe someone had intended for a crow. At least, I hope a crow or fox was the target for his venom and that my beloved dog was a purely accidental victim. If there was a trespasser in the wood, she'd hunt up to him and prance, baying, round him, preventing his escape until someone went to call her off. It was an effective way of clearing the place of uninvited guests.

Doing several series of *One Man and His Dog* has entailed quite a few nights away from home and, as we live in a very deserted spot, I don't like leaving my wife alone. So I decided that Tick's understudy should be another alsatian, which could have the run of the house by day and the yard at night. I took a lot of trouble to find a good one and a senior officer of the Metropolitan Police recommended me to a breeder who produces some of their top police and working trial dogs.

Talking it over with George Inger, the idea was born to do a series for *Animal Magic*, starting with me collecting the pup, and showing how I chose it from the litter. I am so fond of Tick that I was determined not to put her nose out of joint by causing her jealousy, and we thought it would be interesting to see a pup integrated into a family which already included a very favourite dog.

I own a ninety-acre nature reserve and am more or less self-supporting in the number of fowls I keep for eggs and the oven, so that the problems of training a puppy to be steady to deer and poultry could be another aspect. And teaching a dog to see-off strangers – and welcome friends – is also calculated to make dog owners turn on the telly. I explained to the chap who sold me the pup that it was likely to feature on TV so that he was happy to enhance my chances of success by giving me the choice of his very best litter.

Just before we were due to film the collecting of the pup, George telephoned to say that he was moving to another programme but that the series was to go on as arranged.

We struggled through February snow on the Pennine Hills, up to a sombre grey stone house guarded, of course, by alsatians! My litter was nine weeks old, as like as peas in a pod, round and playful and affectionate. I met the owner and sized-up his bitch. I scuffled my feet on the gravel – after the owner had removed Mum! – to see which of the pups came to see what the row was about, and which shied off nervously. None of them was nervous. So we turned them all out to play in the snow and I watched, carefully, to see which were bossy and potential pack leaders, and which would rather be led. Finally, and most important, since the newcomer would have to share our home, I asked Jess to pick as well so that success or failure would be ours, not mine. We chose the boldest, strongest, most friendly little bitch.

Puppies always make compelling television, so we came away with delightful film as well as a pup in which I had high hopes. The filming was not finished for the day because, back at home, we shot the very first meeting between Tick and the young alsatian. That was also delightful because the old bitch could give lessons in good manners to many of her human friends. There was a fair amount of sniffing, a little matronly licking to clean up this brat who was only used to living in outside kennels, but never a growl to throw a slur on her hospitality.

We named the new pup Belle, because she was so beautiful. When she yowled and yelped too much in puppyhood, Bellock, our local Staffordshire word for kicking-up a shindig, was not inappropriate; and when she grows older and starts the serious business of seeing-off strangers, an alternative could be Bella, the Latin name for war.

Next time the camera came, 'Belle' suited her to perfection. She had settled down, without much bellocking, as if she'd been born on the place and she certainly hadn't started to bark at trespassers. All the world was her friend and she exuded good fellowship from whatever angle the cameraman picked to shoot her. By now she was twelve weeks old and she would come when I called her, either sit or lie, whichever I chose to request, and even stay when I left her, provided I didn't go out of sight. But the most exciting thing, in my eyes, was that Tick showed no trace of resentment. The pup was being fed four times a day and, each time I fed her, I made a fuss of Tick, and gave her a scrap from the puppy's plate.

The old dog revelled in being so spoiled, and began to associate the new arrival with pleasant things. Each time I invited her to 'Come and see Belle', she knew she was due for a small prize. For my part I was scrupulously careful never to fuss the pup without making sure the old lady had more than her share too.

Like all puppies, Belle's teeth were needle-sharp and she was inclined to plague everyone and everything with them. Any adult dog with mortal flesh would soon grow tired of that and Tick was no exception. She tolerated her tormentor for quite a while and then tried to get out of the way. If this was impossible, she disciplined her with a practical demonstration that puppy teeth were not the only weapons which could pinch. Hard! The temptation was to stop her biting the pup, which rushed screaming for the sanctuary of her kennel. I never succumbed, but left them to find their own level. Within a couple of days, Belle knew just how far she could go without incurring retribution and, within a week, they were firm friends.

I had been slightly worried when I had heard George Inger was leaving *Animal Magic* and that an unknown new producer was coming up from the big city. New brooms who can't see how to be better, are all too often determined to be different. So, next time I was in the studio at Bristol, I called in the office to establish what the current thinking was about how many items were wanted about my pup's training, and how long each should be. It was important for me to know so that I could formulate a training programme which could be divided into the right number of slots.

I soon heard. George's replacement announced that he didn't want anything at all about dogs. He preferred pumas or jaguars or something exotic. 'In politics,' he said, 'the new government is not bound to honour the commitments of the last. And somebody usually gets hurt.' I am glad I don't often have to deal with politicians who seem to get their finales before their opening curtains!

I couldn't help feeling that Belle and I were not the only losers. It so happened that, at the time, I was bottle-rearing an orphan muntjac deer called (without much originality) Jac(k). He was even smaller than the pup and I waited till he was enthusiastically sucking the teat of his bottle before introducing them. The deer's one-track mind thought only of his grub; he was oblivious to everything outside his bottle. Belle thought the drink smelt uncommonly sweet, so started licking the outside of the teat, and the young deer's mouth, in her efforts to get a share. It would have made compulsive television, and, as she grew older, it was equally fascinating to watch the bitch sublimating her hunting urge, as a collie would do, and showing no real desire to give chase and eat him.

It was also illuminating to discover that Belle's selective breeding has produced guarding impulses as powerful as a collie's urge to shepherd sheep, or a pointer's passion for pointing.

A visitor, introduced by a mutual friend, arrived at Goat Lodge one day and brought a nauseating, ill-disciplined brat along with him. Belle, at the time, was about fourteen weeks old, with teeth as sharp as fish hooks, so I called her to heel. The lad wouldn't stop teasing her, in spite of repeated niggles from his old man, so I let the pup look after herself. Her new-found playmate was bigger and heavier and far more stupid. Next time he tried to bully her she pinched him hard enough to make him retreat, in disorder, and then gave chase as all good police dogs should. When she caught up with him, her instinct was to grab him by the sleeve, just as trained police dogs do in man-work trials, and equally effectively. She improved his manners more in the next ten minutes than his father had done in as many years. Discipline is as vital for boys as it is for young pups. The father gave me an old-fashioned look, presumably for not reprimanding the pup but, as he made no remark, I concluded he was secretly glad to see something knocking some manners into the lad.

Belle is growing up now and is steady to other stock, but I am not yet certain if she will be a success despite her charming nature and great intelligence. The breeders of showdogs are the niggers-in-the-woodpile once more. They have a particularly stupid misnomer called 'Beauty' classes and, in common with other dog show-ers, have bred dogs selectively for looks at the expense of stamina and brains. One of the defects they have produced in alsatians is known as hip dysplasia, which is a deformity of the hip joint that worsens progressively until the wretched beasts are cripples. Unfortunately, the defect does not manifest itself until they are nine or ten months old by which time I, for one, would have become sufficiently involved with a dog to be extremely proud of it, so I am crossing my fingers that young Belle continues to develop as sound as she has started.

The task of televising *One Man and His Dog* is quite different from the difficulties posed by other breeds. With sheepdog trials, the action all happens in a relatively small area that could be covered by several cameras shooting simultaneously. With hound-trailing, the hounds do most of their deeds of daring out of sight of the spectators. By coincidence, I was also involved with this very different sport quite close to Loweswater, where we ran the second series of sheepdog trials.

That was the only similarity. The hound-trailing began in an arena, where the crowd could see the start, and then the hounds streamed off up the fell side, following the scent left behind by two trail layers. This led them up to the summit of Melbreak. They streamed along the tops where we could glimpse them occasionally through powerful binoculars as they appeared jumping over a stone wall or breasting a precipitous slope. The course they followed was about ten miles long so that they were away from the arena for anything up to forty-five minutes, during most of which they were completely out of sight.

Then, as the trail approached its climax, a shiver passed through the crowd and necks craned up in the direction from which the first hound was expected to appear. Enthusiasm and local knowledge was such, that the regulars could not only spot the hounds, but identify the leaders with their naked eyes before I could be certain that they were hounds not sheep, even with the aid of my binoculars. Once they were in sight of the finish, the excitement surged to a

133

crescendo as the hounds streamed down the fell side towards the natural green amphitheatre where such lakeland sports are held. Bookmakers bellowed odds against the hound they hoped – or feared – would win. Owners went berserk, waving gaudy rags, like seconds in a boxing ring. They yelled and whistled themselves into purple fits, while the hounds waiting their turn to run a trail, bayed defiance at their panting rivals.

I know of no sport which can incite phlegmatic Englishmen to strip off their inhibitions so brazenly. Translating such a steamy atmosphere to an oblong television screen is as different from planting impressions of the quiet sport of sheepdog trialling as bullfighting is from the contemplative art of fishing.

In a sheepdog trial, it is vital to portray the spontaneous interplay between shepherd and sheep and dog. If one panics or triumphs, viewers wonder what effect it has had on the others. There is no betting nor yelling nor emotional outbursts. The most abandoned man round a trial course will do no more than clap politely to indicate that he has appreciated the sophisticated control of a brilliant shepherd and his dog. The advanced technique of video tape, feeding six simultaneous pictures to the screen – and mind – of one producer, is the perfect medium for depicting such a sport.

But it wouldn't work with this hound trail, where half the action takes place three or four miles away on the other side of a mountain. All there is to see from the arena is the hullabaloo when thirty straining hounds are loosed, sixty seconds' worth of jockeying as they clamber up the fell side, and even greater pandemonium for less time still when they return.

The route they run is determined by the trail layers who start off simultaneously from the farthest point on the course. They set off, in opposite directions, each dragging his noisome bundle, soaked in a malodorous aniseed mixture which will leave a trail hounds can follow, flat out, without pausing to puzzle where their quarry went. Because they set off simultaneously, in opposite directions, the trail layers should arrive at the arena at about the same time. Lest the hounds wind the one that is approaching the finish and set off the wrong way round the course he stops about a quarter of a mile away. The other man comes on down to where each owner is holding his hound, ready to slip him when the starter drops his flag.

The moment hounds see the trail layer, they give tongue. They bay and scream with passion, as though they'd eat him, so that the start of a hound trail provides some of the most thrilling moments on television. When the flag drops, they surge off and envelop him in snarling, writhing, straining muscle – but it is not the trail layer they are after. It is not even the evil-smelling bundle that he drags behind him. They are simply mad to race each other along the trail he has laid. They go round and past him in a baying pack which gradually strings-out as the leaders race ahead through rushing mountain rivers, over foot-punishing rocky scree, over stone walls, through woods and bracken and over the heather-topped heights. The first dog home scoops the major prize – and usually far more than that in side bets.

No Simon Truck would be any good to give an overall picture of such a contest, so Brian Robins, the producer of *Getaway*, gave himself a bird's-eye view by installing a camera in a helicopter. It flew low over hounds, following smoothly where they struggled, fifty feet below it, in lung-bursting efforts to climb up the mountain-sides. It got ahead of the leader so that it could look back through a telephoto lens and take shots of hounds approaching, then circled round to collect reverse angle shots as they disappeared over a wall.

The trail crossed several roads so a Land-Rover was sent up to get close-up shots as hounds approached, crossed and left it, then motored on to the next crossing place to repeat the manoeuvre. Other cameras in the area built up the atmosphere by filming spectators and owners, bookies and visitors. They shot pictures of the Cumberland wrestling, foot races and terrier shows that filled the gaps while hounds were out of sight.

There was no training to depict, in the sense that Glyn Jones educated his sheepdogs, because these hounds just went like hell along the trail the moment they were slipped. They didn't even need to have sensitive noses, because the scent left by the trail layers was so rank that I imagine it could have been followed by a peke with a cold in its head! But there was a great deal of training in the athletic sense. My experience of when my lurcher folded-up coursing a hare on a hot day and, later, when Glyn Jones was training his pup, had driven home the danger of running dogs in great heat. These trail-hounds compound the peril by being sent, at break-neck speed, up mountains in high summer.

They can only sweat through tongue and pads, so the owners shave off their coats to keep them as cool as possible. When they are not running, they rug them up in flannel coats like whippets. They take precautions to see that they don't carry a drachm of surplus fat, because it is the fat that builds up heat and the fat that they sweat off. So every rib of a trail-hound sticks out as if he'd just done a spell at Belsen and, if you handle one, you will discover he is as hard as a drum because he carries nothing surplus to the muscle and sinew that drives him on.

In order to get a dog as thin as that, without sacrificing his strength, it is vital to give him the most nourishing food imaginable. Each owner has his own secret recipe, but many use eggs and sherry and the finest steak. 'Fed like a fighting cock' could well be translated to 'Fed like a trail-hound', since both need maximum strength and fitness combined with the minimum surplus fat.

In filming the specialised feeding and training such an exacting sport demands, it occurred to us that the men who owned the dogs must be pretty fit as well. After a hard day's work farming or shepherding on the fells, they take their dogs several miles on hard roads 'to get their muscle up and their feet hard'.

It is not a race where winners take rich prizes, but such an enthusiasts' sport, with the bedlam of a close-run finish as climax, is ideal for television. The pleasure of such occasions is that genuine countrymen, willing to take enormous trouble to amuse themselves, rather than paying to be amused, can't fail to come across as the truly charming folk they are.

Years before I ever saw competitive hound-trailing, I had a lot of fun with trail-hounds of a different sort. Reg Wright, a tremendous character who is an old friend of mine, claims to be able to hunt anything from a mouse to a man. He keeps terriers for ratting and bolting foxes, so I reckon his claim of catching a mouse is fair enough; and he keeps a pack of mixed beagles and basset hounds – officially for hunting hare but by no means averse to killing a fox, if it's stupid enough to get in their way. But my love are his bloodhounds – with which he is only too willing to fulfill his claim to be able to hunt a man!

They are a formidable sight. Ten or twelve couples of black-and-tan brutes with voices as deep as a peal of cathedral bells – and far more inviting to my untutored ears. The first time I saw them hunt was a marvellous summer evening – and they were hunting human prey. Some stout-hearted chap, who set off across the dew-soaked fields, did about a three-mile run and, an hour after he returned, Reg showed the hounds his jacket and sent them off. They tore down the path where he had started, crossed the next field through the same gap in the hedge and disappeared over the skyline in precisely the same spot. Long after they disappeared, we could hear the chimes of their cry, echoing across the evening countryside.

After a bit, I noticed Reg was uneasy, and asked him why. 'Well, Joe went right-handed,' he said 'and I can hear them speaking over there.' 'Speaking' was an understatement. They were baying louder than the chorus from *The Hound of the Baskervilles* – and mixed in with their sonorous music were high-pitched feminine cries for 'Help'. Reg disappeared after them like a whippet and I followed, tentatively, fearful of what I should see.

After Reg's friend had laid his trail, a courting couple had crossed it on the way to their trysting place. Bloodhounds, of course, should ignore such distractions and continue to puzzle out their original line, but these bloodhounds did not run according to form. Some rebel among them preferred the alien scent and, forsaking his original track, set off in full cry after the strangers. The rest of the pack lifted their heads, hesitated, and fell in with the false leader. The trysting place was soon discovered and the trespassers vanished beneath a heaving mass of slobbering hounds, each competing for the honour of kissing the bride.

The young woman took it amiss and nothing that Reg could say would convince her that they were intent only on showing their affection – so I doubt if she did much courting on his farm again.

I was delighted by the whole display and asked if we could run a film for television – a proper run, of course, without changing the line to hunt a courting couple. From television's point of view, the task was not only easy but very spectacular. The whole run was assembled artificially in a series of relatively short bursts. To start off, the hounds were filmed in kennels, and later spilling out of the hound van to assemble as a pack at a conventional meet.

Then the trail-layer ran off and was filmed disappearing past some telegenic landmark. Hounds were shown their quarry's jacket – which he'd left behind – the huntsman blew his horn and yelled, 'Hunt 'im, fellers, hunt 'im, hunt 'im, hunt 'im', and the hounds screamed away in ecstasy. It was quite impressive.

When they'd gone just out of sight, the hounds were stopped, brought back to the start, and the whole sequence was repeated with the camera in front, so that the producer had film of quarry and hounds, going over the same ground, shot from two directions. This gave him a sequence as long or as short as he liked. Hounds won't hunt the same quarry over the same ground too often but, if more variety of shots was needed, it was quite easy to get someone else to run the same line as the first quarry did. The hounds then appeared against the same background from a variety of interesting new angles, which were edited into the main theme.

Reg conned me into acting as quarry and I can testify that, however harmless bloodhounds are supposed to be, he would be an unimaginative dolt if the hair on the nape of his neck didn't rise when he heard them in full cry and realised it was him they were after. I knew they were after me because, to make his picture more vivid, George Inger, the producer, wanted hounds and me in view at the same time for the last part of the trail.

We did a nice film for *Animal Magic* which I enjoyed because Johnny Morris, who introduces it, is one of the pleasantest, most professional chaps I know to work with. Then I was asked to do another for one of the news magazines.

Newsmen are a breed apart. They spend their lives telling stories from all over the world but I doubt if they ever listen to them because it is wonderful what they don't know. When I called in to discuss filming bloodhounds, the first question was 'What do bloodhounds hunt?' 'Man,' I said, laconically. A long and pregnant pause while his tortuous mind coiled itself round possible 'new' angles. Newsmen always like 'new 'angles and they have their own jargon for them. A 'searching' interview means being impertinently curious about someone else's business. A 'hard' interview means being bloody impertinent, probably because it has been decided to send-up the victim and make him look stupid because he doesn't conform to newsmen's trendy views.

Since there was no obvious hard or searching approach to bloodhound trailing and nothing to 'knock', he thought it rather dull. Then a gleam of cunning lit his eye. An idea had filtered through to cap his predecessor's headline proclaiming 'Man bites

Dog'. 'Hunts man, you said?' I nodded. 'Would they hunt a woman?'

'If you could get one to lay them a line,' I answered.

'You're on. Get her.'

Monosyllabic, these news chaps. No wasted words or waffle!

As it happened, I knew a very good-looking girl who whipped-in for a local pack of beagles. She could run all day and finish looking as fresh and attractive as when she started. I rang her up. 'Ever seen blood-hounds at work?' I asked innocently. She said she'd never had the chance and would be delighted to come when I told her a pack was meeting shortly at my place and that we were going to film it for television. I omitted to tell her that she was cast for stardom.

The night before the meet I rang her up and told her that we were having a bit of difficulty about getting someone fit enough to run the line. Would she be prepared to step in? All it amounted to, I said, was running a predetermined line, coming back to the start from where she could watch them puzzling out the trail that she had laid. And I asked her to come in leather shoes, not wellingtons, as rubber masks the scent.

We'd picked a lovely hill top for start and finish, so that we could look across a green and fertile valley in the vale of the Trent. I asked her to run down the left-hand hedgeside to a ploughed field in the distance, work her way a hundred yards across to the right, come nearly back to us, but then to turn away again, into the distance, where she could make another great loop before returning to the start.

The purpose of this was so that one camera could follow her course from the top of the hill, while another, down in the centre, could film her and the hounds coming past, but would have plenty of time to move over a hundred yards each time she doubled back on herself; this would give lots of close-up shots.

Finally, I told her that we should like her to stop fifty yards away from us when she had nearly finished, and only come up to us when the stage manager gave her the cue.

'Why do you want me to do that?' she asked. The producer explained that he wanted hounds to catch up with her, in close-up, right in front of his camera. 'Catch up with me? Good God, what happens then?' she cried. Reg Wright stepped in to assure her that his hounds were the most demonstrative, affectionate darlings which might smother her with smelly kisses, but would never bare a fang in anger.

I didn't tell her that the master and I had agreed, in private, that one should have the mask and the other the brush. It might have put her off!

Filming wild animals is quite a different matter because there's no chance of persuading them to do the job twice for reverse angles, or to wait for 'action' till the camera is set up, and the sound man has a tape on his spool, and everything is turning over. That doesn't mean that it's easy to drub such basic facts into every producer's mind.

Some years ago, I hand-reared a perfectly delightful roe deer which stayed as tame as a robin for her ten-year lifespan, although she lived wild in the wood. Chatting in the BBC bar, I happened to mention to a shiny new producer that 'my roe deer comes to my study window, at eleven sharp every day, for a biscuit, when I have my morning coffee'. I soon regretted my stupidity.

He immediately bought me a pint, asked for more

details and, before I knew what hit me, he'd commissioned an item for a magazine programme he was producing. A week or so later, he turned up with a cameraman, assistant cameraman, sound engineer, electrician and dolly bird with a clip board. He was obviously a glutton for action and had hardly consumed the statutory coffee and biscuits before he was raring to go. He surveyed the study and told Sparks to get it lit while he decided where the deer would come.

I was by no means sure that she would come at all with a battery of floodlights glaring at her over my shoulder. The edge of the wood is about fifty yards from the window and I soon located her, lying-up in a patch of bracken, not too far from the edge.

Meanwhile the young boss-man had sited his camera, assistant cameraman and fellow with the microphone at right angles to my window and no more than four feet from it. 'I want the deer to walk out of the wood there,' he said, indicating a nut bush with a pretty background. 'Then get her to come directly towards the camera, till she is in front of the open window. When she gets here' – and he planted a symbolic pebble for her turning point – 'when she gets here, call her and give her the biscuit so that we can come into close-up on your head and hers.'

He didn't really look stupid, so I could only conclude he was either utterly ignorant or pulling my leg. I played it deadpan and asked if I should give her a chocolate biscuit or would it be better to stick to plain, in case it offended the food-for-the-Third-World fanatics? He wasn't joking. So I had to make up my mind whether or not to tell him the facts of life; I opted for giving it a spin to see how I got on.

Jess came to the rescue, as she so often does. She

143

feeds the stock when I'm away, exercises the dogs, locks the hens up – and copes with the eccentricities of such young enthusiasts with tolerance and good humour beyond my ken. Moving with the stealth of a chameleon, she let the roe deer taste the sweetness of life by licking the chocolate off a biscuit. Having whetted her appetite, she retreated towards the camera, just enough off line to be comfortably out of shot. When the deer was opposite my window she faded from view by merging with the galaxy of strangers – and left it to me to call her in.

They might never have been there. The little doe turned unselfconsciously to me, put two feet on the step and shared my biscuit as if there wasn't a soul in sight. Jess and I were duly chuffed, feeling the warm glow of those who have just excelled themselves. We waited for *our* verbal reward.

'Not bad,' said the young man. 'Hang around while I put the camera at the edge of the wood and we'll repeat it from the reverse angle.'

As gently as possible, I explained that we had just achieved the near impossible by persuading a virtually wild deer to leave the sanctuary of her wood and approach a gaggle of weirdly dressed strangers, whirring cameras and flashing high-powered lights. To persuade the deer to allow any stranger to get between it and safety, cutting off its line of retreat, would need more than a magnum of miracles. He couldn't persuade a hand-reared lamb to do that – so we parted with the mutual conviction we had wasted each other's time.

I suppose that geese are even more difficult because I know nothing wilder than a wild wild goose. I had been hearing tales for years about a character called

Kensie Thorpe, 'the goose man', but had not had the luck to meet him. His parish was the saltings of the Wash and some said he was the perfect guide for anyone wanting to go onto the treacherous marshes, sacrosanct to duck and geese, curlew and sandpipers and seals. Photographers said there was nobody like Kensie to show them where to shoot – and so did wildfowlers with guns.

And, if rumours were to be trusted, plenty of local landowners would testify that a litter of foxes or a coven of cats were innocents compared to Kensie – who could charm the pheasants out of the trees by the sweetness of his voice. If Lincolnshire poachers were your cup of tea, Kensie was said to be the grand-daddy of them all.

We first came face to face at the Game Fair at Tatton Park. I was working for Tony Parkin, who produces the farming programme that goes out, live, on steam radio first thing on Saturday mornings. My job was to find four likely, diverse characters and to chat them up in order to give a thumbnail sketch of what the Game Fair is about. I have no idea who three of my folk were – they have faded to oblivion. But I shall never forget old Kensie Thorpe.

I found him on the WAGBI stand, which is the honeypot that draws all shooting men. Most wild-fowlers shoot geese by digging a pit in the mud when the tide is out, and hiding there in the hopes that an unwary goose will pass within gunshot overhead. The clever locals know the traditional flight lines so that they site their 'hides' where there is a reasonable chance of success.

Kensie went far better than that. He dug a pit in a good spot and then gilded the gingerbread by imi-tating the cry of a wild goose so faithfully that he could literally call them to him. Or so the rumour had it.

When I discovered him, he was surrounded by a gaggle of gaping gunners, giving demonstrations of his repertoire of calls. After talking to him for a while, I was left in no doubt that he'd be a natural for the programme the following morning. Whether the calls worked or not, they sounded lifelike and there was no doubt that he could spin a marvellous yarn.

Just before we went, live, on the air, I asked him how he wanted me to introduce him. Did he want to be called a guide on the marshes, or a poacher, or wildfowler – or what? I didn't want to insult him by suggesting that he *was* a poacher, but it was important to find out what his reaction, on the air, would be if I suggested it. So I included it in my catalogue as a throwaway.

'I don't mind, sir,' he said. 'Call me what you like.'

I introduced him as a wildfowler and he gave superb imitations of wild geese and curlews, and oyster catchers and dunlin. When he'd gone on for a bit, I interrupted and pointed out that all his renditions were waterfowl or waders. Did he do any land-birds? 'I'll do you a pheasant, sir,' he said and did a lifelike imitation of the 'Cock-up, Cock-up' that the old cocks cry when flying up to roost.

'That's fine,' I said, 'but what on earth time do you shoot your pheasants? That one was just going up to roost, wasn't he?'

'He was,' Kensie replied, 'I likes to get 'em silhouetted against the moon, sir!'

'Do you, indeed? And have you ever been caught poaching?'

'Lots of times, sir,' he said, and it was only then

that the significance of his automatic suffix Sir, filtered through my mind.

'I was caught twice on the King's estate at Sandringham. But I haven't been to see the Queen. Yet.'

'Follow that', as they say!

We got on so well that I persuaded Peter Crawford, who produces *The Country Game* and other country programmes, to put him to the test and see if he really could call geese with a camera present to bear witness to the fact.

We assembled on the saltings of the Wash when the tide was going out. There were thousands of acres of black glutinous mud, topped with tufts of unappetising weed. The whole area was interspersed with a sort of varicose network of little channels, which drained water to the tide line on the ebb but filled long before water showed elsewhere when the tide turned to come in. It would have been all too easy without a guide who knew the area as well as the veins on his hand, to get cut off and marooned by deep water that literally crept up behind one. There was no such worry with Kensie, and we all walked out about a mile, to within a hundred yards of the tide, which had not yet finished ebbing. We were loaded like camels with photographic gear, Kensie humping, in addition, a useful-looking spade.

When we got to the spot he wanted, he cut gooey chunks of stinking mud and dropped them in a nearby channel, which was about four feet deep, until he had cut it off from the landward side completely. This dammed back the trickle of water still seeping down to the sea. Then he blocked it off about six feet to the seaward side, making a muddy – but relatively dry – pit about four feet deep, six feet long and two

147

feet wide. He camouflaged the edges with tussocks of grass and weed.

The cameraman had filmed him while he did it so that it would be obvious to viewers how the pit Kensie and I would be peering from had been made. Finally he dug a precisely similar pit, about twenty yards behind, to camouflage the camera crew while they filmed what we were at.

We settled down to watch and, within a quarter of an hour, a party of corpulent seals were lying, bellies up on the mud, no more than eighty yards away, sunning themselves with the gay abandon of ladies on the beach at Blackpool. Far, far out, the tiny specks on the sandbanks were geese and waders in safe sanctuary, out of gunshot range.

Each time we shuffled about in our muddy den, a new layer of stinking slime coagulated on our clothes till we needed no other disguise. But the continuous stream of rare and beautiful birds flying over us was more than compensation.

At last the tide turned and gradually submerged the sandbanks. The seals slid into the cool water and the wildfowl rose in relays and migrated to the next bank nearer shore. Some of them flew quite a long way towards us and Kensie began imitating their cries to decoy them nearer.

The camera behind us, literally at salting level, could see only our heads, as if we had been buried up to the neck and left for crabs and conger eels to consume alive. Most of the birds were flying parallel to the tideline, directly across us, so the effects, if any, of Kensie's avian entreaties were recorded on film.

His confidence was justified, for he was extremely successful. Time after time, birds flying across our bows checked and wheeled down to see what he was shouting the odds about. If we had had guns, we could have shot a hamperful and, as it was, the camera got a far more satisfying haul of geese, redshanks and curlew which left us their images and escaped with their lives.

It was a superb demonstration of the sophisticated hunter's craft which made it possible to film more shy birds before the tide came in than we could have done ourselves if we had hung around for weeks.

'Manipulating 'animals for television, whether by the sportsman's art or the naturalist's science, can be an enthralling business. My wood, of about ninety acres, is on the edge of the old forest of Needwood, most of which has been felled and replanted with conifers. Since I own about forty acres of ancient standing oak wood, I start off with the advantage that a great many birds and animals – particularly fallow deer, regard it as a pretty desirable residence, especially at acorn harvest time. One way of helping to pay for its up-keep is to make it attractive for television producers as well as wildlife. So I have tried to 'manipulate' my wild deer so that they are relatively easy – and therefore cheap – to film.

The most important step to take was to see that it is completely free from disturbance. Animals which have to be constantly alert for fools with unruly brats or dogs, are difficult to stalk with a camera. Even well-behaved, innocent country lovers can empty a small wood like mine if they split up, so that some pass one side of a party of deer and some the other. One thing that no shy animal will tolerate is having his retreat cut off – as the young producer discovered when he tried to interpolate his camera between my roe deer and the wood. The only reverse angle he got was her backside vanishing at high velocity!

The next thing I did was to intersperse the wood with grassy rides, not only to act as feed for the deer but as tracks to walk round, or drive round when necessary. By going round them regularly with the dogs – and keeping out of the wood itself – it is possible to engender such a sense of security that I can pass within twenty or thirty yards of perfectly wild deer without disturbing them.

Finally, I have been able to persuade them to come more or less where I want by 'baiting' selected areas with wheat or flaked maize, and they even feed from the bird table within a few feet of the sitting-room window.

At this stage, I was astonished to discover that they appeared oblivious to artificial light. They ignored the house and yard lights so that I put up a halogen quartz floodlight, which illuminates the paddock and woodland edge. They still took no notice – nor do hares or foxes – and we have been able to augment my amateur lighting with full television lighting and film them through the window!

But it isn't always possible to influence the creatures one wishes to film so that all one can do is either wait or know exactly where to look.

I have worked a lot for Dilys Breese who produces *Wildlife* and *Living World* for steam radio. So when she invited me to take part in a television programme called *In Deepest Britain*, I was naturally delighted – until I heard the details.

The idea was to go out with two other naturalists to an interesting piece of country for a day's filming, and film what we saw. She innocently invited me to suggest the venue. I should have told any other producer that my diary was full because I know enough about wild places to realise how easy it is to go out on one's own and hardly see a living thing all day. At least, certainly not anything worth filming and, even more certainly, not when accompanied by the razzmatazz of a film crew. But Dilys is different. She is about as gluttonous for work as Philip Gilbert, and I know no producer I respect more highly.

So I suggested Cannock Chase in June, and accepted her invitation. There are a lot of deer and a wide variety of other wildlife on Cannock Chase – and there is also Gerald Springthorpe. Gerald, who is a Forestry Commission Game Warden, has been a friend of mine for more than thirty years. He has forgotten more practical field craft than most of the boffins will ever know, and we got working on the project a week or so before Dilys was due to descend on us with her crew.

In the centre of the Chase there is a large observation hut on stilts in front of which Gerald has cut radial rides where deer can feed. More important from our viewpoint, where they can be seen feeding. He has put up nest boxes around, and planted food plants for as many species as possible; he chose the site for the hut in a favourite area for foxes and badgers. The hut is rented to the public by the Forestry Commission – but we monopolised it for a day's filming just when we calculated most fallow deer would be dropping their fawns.

It worked like a charm. Stephen Sutton, one of the other naturalists went up with me at dawn to discover what there was to see, and the whole cast paraded precisely on cue. We saw a fallow doe with a fawn so young that it didn't know where the milk bar was and kept nuzzling at the wrong end. We saw pheasants and foxes, turtle doves and small birds, so that there wasn't a dull moment.

Then we walked on the Chase, but we took a carefully worked-out route where Gerald and I knew there was good copy – if only we could uncover it. We found another fawn, dropped a few hours earlier and still relying on camouflage rather than flight, and we were able to film it in close-up without disturbing it. We found birds' nests and exotic insects and, most exciting for me because I don't really like snakes, we found an adder sunning herself on a sandy bank. She almost slid up to the camera lens, giving us a superb close-up that still makes my flesh creep.

I had feared disaster but, partly due to Gerald's local knowledge and partly to luck, it worked out fine in the end. But it was conventional stuff compared to *Badger Watch*.

Badger Watch was a programme in which I was invited to take part by Peter Bale. He had earlier produced 'The Night of the Fox' in *The World About Us* series, a programme about foxes, shot very largely in the dark.

There was no commercially available equipment that was suitable for televising in the dark and he wanted to record the behaviour of foxes during hours of their activity when they are normally invisible. So the backroom boys of the BBC dreamed-up a technique for televising objects illuminated by infra-red light that is not visible to our eyes.

Better still, they did not dredge up their brainchild from a bottomless barrel of golden guineas. They fashioned the prototype from clapped-out silent cooling fans and a redundant monochrome caption camera!

The infra-red light emitted by their gadget was invisible to human – and presumably foxy – eyes, but conjured up a perfect picture in the darkness. The name, 'Eye in the Night,' was a very fair description of their infra-red-sensitive electronic camera. The whole theory is far beyond my comprehension, but the outcome was that they were able to record behaviour that was taking place in what seemed to be total darkness.

The fox film, which was about foxes in controlled conditions, was so successful that Peter Bale decided to observe a sett of wild badgers and to televise the picture he got by infra-red light, live, in a series of programmes transmitted on consecutive nights. I was one of the team of observers invited to comment on what we saw.

The location was a wooded valley in Gloucestershire which was particularly densely populated by badgers. A platform on scaffolding had been erected where the sett could be observed a few yards away, and two cameras were mounted on the platform. These were connected to a scanner about three hundred yards away and monitors and camera controls were installed in a nearby caravan. The cameras were worked from the caravan by remote control and they could be raised or lowered, 'panned' to right or left or zoomed into close-unp when the badgers' nearest human neighbour was so far away that they could neither hear nor smell them.

The sett we were to watch had eight entrances, each of which had been numbered on a plan, and bugged with a microphone, numbered to correspond with its plan location. Each microphone was connected to an instrument above the sound engineer's head which indicated when the microphone was working.

I arrived, on the first night, at about six o'clock and was horrified to see someone apparently tramping about over the entrances to the sett. I was told that heavy rain had caused a bit of crackle in the microphones down the sett entrance and that he was servicing them!

I had made nightly observations on the badgers in my wood for five consecutive years. My badgers were hand-reared and remained tame enough to handle for most of the time, although I had established them at complete liberty. Yet if a stranger interfered with their sett after tea time, there was little hope of seeing them that night. So I took a jaundiced view of the prospects of having anything to describe when we went, live, on the air at about eleven that night.

We settled in the caravan long before we were due to begin, our eyes glued to the monitor screen, relaying what the automated cameras could 'see' of the sett and its surroundings.

There was too much evidence of human interference for my liking. The scaffold camera tower must have given the whole ground a good drumming when it was erected. A microphone down each hole, reeking with the breath of previous human performers, was enough to make any badger quit for sweeter lodgings. Stinking rubber cables snaked from cameras to caravan across the valley; and a crew, almost the size of the mob for *One Man and His Dog*, were bivouacked where eddies on the evening air must have proclaimed our presence to every brock for miles around.

The only thing in our favour was that the miracle

of infra-red rays, which revealed all to the camera, left the place apparently as dark as a bag.

Once having been bitten by such a pessimistic bug, my mind wrestled with other unpleasantries. This was to be the first time wild badgers had ever been seen on live television, shown on the screen the instant they appeared in the wild. The programme was scheduled to divulge badger secrets for four consecutive nights. So there had been a great deal of publicity and ballyhoo about it. The planners had prudently scheduled it for about eleven o'clock at night presumably because, if it fell flat on its face, as seemed ominously likely, viewers could switch off without missing subsequent programmes. What they seemed to have overlooked was that anyone who had bothered to hang around so long, obviously wanted to see badgers very badly and would feel pretty cheated if all they got for their money was wretched 'experts' explaining what they might have seen if things had gone according to plan.

Resisting the temptation to sneak away and drown our sorrows in the nearest local, we put brave faces on it. Almost before the light had faded, there was a succession of thumps and bangs on one of the subterranean microphones and a needle in the bank of instruments kicked and convulsed as erratically as a seismograph in an earthquake.

'He's coming out of tunnel four,' hissed the sound engineer. The automated cameras swung and focused, zooming-in as a badger's black-and-white-striped head surfaced bang on cue. If only he would take a rest and repeat his performance two and a half hours later, when we went on the air, he would make history by being the first of his kind to make his début on live television.

The next hour or so was hell. Badgers popped up out of all sorts of holes, disappearing backwards, dragging bedding down to their dens. Strange badgers appeared from beyond our field of view and entered our sett, from which thunderous growls and grunts emerged in torrents of foul language. We saw badgers plucking reluctant, elastic worms from amongst the roots, and cubs playing with the boisterous enthusiasm of prep school kids succumbing to their first temptation to beat each other up at Rugby football.

Our frustration was that the run-up to the programme was packed with action and we were only too conscious that the meagre ten minutes we were allotted on the screen could so easily be blank and sterile. Peter Bale was tele-recording what we saw so that, if the worst came to the worst, he could do a sort of action replay, but it would have sapped us of the challenge of spontaneous comment if he had.

By sheer good luck, the badgers turned up trumps. At various times during the week, they demonstrated the domestic art of making badger beds and feeding and playing and kicking out trespassers, utterly oblivious that millions of human eyes could well be watching them.

One of the most exciting incidents of all only concerned them indirectly. In a great beech tree over the sett, a young tawny owl sat at the mouth of his nesting hole, almost ready to fledge. Then, one night, while the camera watched him, he launched himself into space, only to discover that he was not as good at flying as he thought.

He belly-flopped to earth, right at the mouth of a badger hole and we held our breath lest he was eaten before his life had really begun.

The suspense seemed eternal, but he scuffled to

the foot of an elm tree, grabbed the bark with feet and hooked bill and heaved himself up to the safety of a branch using his three-point suspension with all the skill of a veteran mountaineer with crampons or a parrot doing acrobatics in his cage.

It was literally a cliff-hanger in every sense, and no ornithologist that I have spoken to knew that owlets, unable to fly, were versatile enough to improvise such a novel method of escape.

It was one of the magic moments that puts the interminable waits and mad panics of television into perspective, and not least of the rewards was the delightful sketch of the badger, drawn for me by a viewer simply because she'd enjoyed the programme.

The sad postscript is that every badger who used the sett we showed on television was subsequently gassed by Ministry of Agriculture officials. The Ministry vets contend that badgers can cantract bovine TB from infected cattle and spread it to healthy herds.

The evidence is purely circumstantial and, in any case, any competent naturalist knows that an attractive area denuded of a species of wildlife quickly refills from surrounding areas. So the Ministry's action is as futile as Canute sweeping back the waves and far more damaging to our native wildlife.

"... on 'the box'..."

Chapter Eight

'THAT'LL DO!'

Television is usually fun in prospect and, occasionally, in retrospect. It can be sheer hell at the time. The moment of truth dawned on me when Simon Betts, our stage manager, called to pick me up and ferry me to the Lake District to record the first series of *One Man and His Dog*. My broken arm was too painful for driving and, when we arrived, we found the hotel dejected and empty because everyone had gone down to the trials field.

Eric was smiting wooden posts into the ground with a sledgehammer as a precise location for the hurdles, or 'gates', he wanted the sheep driven through. Philip was lining-up cameras, though I marvelled that they could focus through the clouds of acrid smoke that hung as a halo round Eric's woolly head. Gerry was dishing out sheaves of notes, running orders and draft scripts to members of the crew. Everyone was up to their eyes in it except Simon and me.

The little-cog-in-a-big-wheel syndrome hit me again. I looked round the field at the scanner and caravans, the camera tenders and generators and video tape vans, all parked as immaculately as in a military encampment.

A hundred yards away, the trials field layout was being battered into impeccable order by Eric and his gang. There was a pen at the top of the field for holding sheep that had not been used for a trial – and another, at the bottom, for those that had. The mess tent was already clattering with crockery and tea was steaming in an urn. An electrician was fitting up a monitor in the adjoining tent so that the competitors could retire to watch what was on the screen.

Having nothing better to do, I speculated on the capital cost involved but, being a bit slaphappy with decimals, I wasn't sure whether to tot-up results in hundreds of thousands or millions of pounds. The point was only academic, but the mood I was in emphasised that somebody had gambled such big sums on the series that I would be in a hot seat if I bodged it up. My confidence plummeted to zero. The summits of the hills faded in the grey mist to sombre shadows on Lake Buttermere, and reflected my pessimism. All that was needed was a scud of drizzling rain to douse my spirits irretrievably.

Dinner at the hotel did little to restore them. Philip maintained the same cheerful façade through thick and thin, bolstering the morale of his team as all born leaders do. But eyeing him surreptitiously, I got the feeling that even he was wondering if he had bitten off more than he could chew. There comes a limit to the quality of silk purses a fistful of sows' ears will make, however skilful the seamster may be!

Sitting opposite to me was the girl with brilliant

green feline eyes, so luminous that I wondered if they would outshine the figures on her alarm clock if she wakened in the night. At that stage, I hadn't discovered her trick of dropping spots of colour under her contact lenses.

My attention wandered nearer home when the second course arrived. Soup had been easy enough, but there was no way of dissecting a steak with one arm in a splint. Gerry and Andy Bloomfield, sitting each side of me, came to the rescue. Without any fuss or ostentation, my plate was whipped from under my nose and one or other of them cut up my food and returned it every meal. All I had to do was to stab the chunks with my fork and chobble them down, as the Yankees do. It was typical of the professional approach of everyone in the team. Whatever went awry was put right by anyone able to do so, whether it was his responsibility or not.

On such nights, many of the crew are strangers, so that there is almost the atmosphere of a first day at a new school. Snatches of conversation discover common acquaintances who have worked on previous jobs; folk who have been remembered as worry-guts or bluffers or idlers or, more often, as grand chaps to work with. In my experience, the worst social snobs are people who have least to be snobbish about, and the same applies to television. Second-raters are often so determined to convince the world – and possibly themselves – how good they are that they get heads too big to go through the west end door of a cathedral. The real top-notchers treat everyone as equals.

So the first evening, before a job begins, is a time for mutual probing and testing when so many common factors usually emerge that, by the time the bar

160

shuts, there is an air of good fellowship which sends everyone to bed steeped in optimistic spirits.

I usually wake about four in a strange bed, by which time the euphoria had evaporated. I discovered that the working notes Gerry had sent to introduce the first programme had left an uncomfortable blank in my mind. Philip had painted the pattern he wanted in words that had been crystal clear last time I read them. With ten days' notice, the whole thing had seemed simplicity itself. At dawn on the morning I was to do the job, the whole thing was as cloudy as last night's beer swillings. Getting out of bed, I fumbled the notes from the bottom of my case and was relieved to discover that things were not as gloomy as I feared.

Andy cut up my bacon at breakfast as if there were nothing he would rather do, and Gerry stitched me into my jacket so that my tailor should have paid her for advertising his sartorial excellence on the box.

We were on the trials field by nine, and so were the competitors. This, in itself, was a good omen. Time doesn't matter much to most countrymen. Crops cannot be hurried to ripen, and birth and growth cannot be accelerated because some hustler is losing his cool. I have plenty of friends in quiet places who will interpret 'Be there by nine thirty' as an open invitation to turn up anywhere between eight and ten o'clock. Our chaps were around with half an hour to spare. Everyone congregated in the competitors' tent so that Philip could introduce the people they'd be dealing with. They all knew Eric already, but it was important for them to know that I would be chatting to some of them after they'd won – or lost – and that the stage managers would tell them when to start and where to stop.

161

He explained that the course had been slightly modified from the standard laid down by the International Sheep Dog Society to make it easier to understand on television. Penning the sheep would now be the last part of the trial in order to keep competitors, dogs and sheep static while the score was announced and a mobile camera brought up to cover an interview with the winner. The most tricky change, from the competitor's point of view, was that the course had been foreshortened to avoid dogs and sheep at the far end looking tiny as tomtits on a round of beef. Most of the shepherds were used to the wide spaces of remote hillsides and working sheep in a constricted area demanded different techniques.

Chris Todd, one of the back-room boys, did many jobs unhonoured, uncomplaining and unsung. He appeared, anonymously, on the programme more often than any of the competitors, because Philip used him as the bait to get the more sensitive of his television audience on the hook before a blow was struck. He chose a glorious, wild stretch of scenery to lay his titles over, in the certain knowledge that anyone susceptible to atmosphere was bound to let it run, if only because the beauty of the countryside took their breath away. To make assurance doubly sure, he added movement to his picture in the shape of a shepherd and a collie driving sheep. The original, anonymous one man and his dog! Chris is an international trials winner in his own right, so he was this perfect silent shepherd of the hills to set the scene.

To seal up his package, so that no one who had a soul could resist it, Philip used a signature tune. He browsed through the sound archives in search of a suitably emotive pastoral refrain, but found nothing that satisfied his standards of perfection. So he com-

162

missioned a piece composed by Alec Benson and it was played over the picture of Chris Todd as the introduction every week.

The tune is also called *One Man and His Dog* and, whenever it is played, it will always be associated with wild and beautiful scenery, quiet countrymen and wise dogs. Countless viewers write to know if it has been recorded and where they can buy a copy, but so far they are out of luck. If enough continue to bombard the BBC, perhaps it will be released as a recording in its own right.

George Hutton, who organised the food and drink tent, and the hurdles for obstacles on the course, also provided the sheep. As the chap in charge at the far end of the course, he started each day with enough and some to spare to allow him to turn out five fresh sheep for each competitive run. When the run was over, they were penned at the other end of the field, waiting to be reunited with their fellows at the end of the day and returned to more peaceful pastures. It was a very responsible job. Although all the sheep were collected from the same flock, there was no guarantee that they all came from groups that were used to running together. If one odd stranger was included in a bunch, it might be easier to separate – or shed – because it would be trying to get back to its own cronies. On the other hand, the odd one out might also be harder to drive because there would be less instinct for it to stay in a tight bunch with the rest. George was responsible for garlanding two with red ribbons round their necks – and it was one of these which the competitor had to separate from its fellows.

With such intimate knowledge of the ways of sheep it was vital that competitors should like and respect him – and there has not been a single whisper of complaint in all the series.

Before it was possible to record the first of the trials, it was necessary to have a rehearsal so that the cameramen would know what to expect. They had no idea how fast the sheep would move or how much they were likely to spread out, or precisely where the limpid mountain light could be exploited to produce peerless pictures. They wanted to see if the dogs were tall enough to be visible in the long grass at the far end of the field without raising the cameras, and whether spectators on a path down one side would obtrude on their picture. Only when they had seen this at first-hand could they make final plans with Philip in the confidence that they could contribute their fair share to the programme.

Chris Todd helped out. His dog, which lavished such demonstrative affection on him in the opening titles, demonstrated in no uncertain way that he was not just an ornament. He put his bunch of sheep through their paces with the discipline of an old-time sergeant major, not only showing the cameramen all they needed to know, but setting a standard that competitors would be hard put to follow.

That done, all was set to go. The course was laid out so that the judges' tent was in a direct line with the shepherd's starting peg, a pair of sheep hurdles (the artificial 'gate' in the centre of the course) and a peg in the distance where the sheep would start. Two more 'gates' had been placed, about a hundred yards apart, at each side and half-way up the course, while there was a pen made of four hurdles to one side of the shepherd and a 'shedding ring' about thirty yards from the pen. The shedding ring was clearly marked out by a trail of sawdust.

The scale of the whole thing would have been difficult to show in a single shot with a camera, but Andy's artist's impression made it all crystal clear.

When Philip was ready to record a run, he told his stage manager over the walkie-talkie, to ask Chris Todd to get his sheep in position and warn the first shepherd to be ready. As if by magic, five sheep appeared from their straw bale pen at the top end of the field and Chris coaxed and wheedled them close to their starting peg. It looked simple enough, but these hill sheep are edgy creatures, subject to fits of blind panic almost as bad as genuinely wild creatures would suffer. One sudden false move by Chris or his dog could have stampeded them so that the wretched dog which had to drive them round the formalised course would have been at an unfair disadvantage. As an international champion, Chris had been through the hoop himself and realised his responsibility. He allowed the sheep to drift haphazardly from their pen, and waited for them to settle down to sample the lush green turf which they must have reckoned five-star grub compared to the arid feg of their spartan fellside grazing. As soon as they had settled comfortably, his dog slunk round them, slyly as a shadow, keeping his distance so as not to startle them. Almost imperceptibly, he inched a little closer until they took the hint and drifted towards the starting peg.

When Philip could see that they were headed gently in the right direction and would be close to the peg in a few seconds, he radioed to Simon to send the first competitor to his starting peg.

The opening shot picked up the shepherd waiting by the judges' tent and then walking out onto the field with his collie at his heels. He paused, for a

165

while, to make sure the dog had seen his quarry and then set him off to gather them. The dog sped off, tail tucked in, skimming smoothly but not directly at the sheep because that would have scattered them in all the wrong directions. He slipped, instead, along the very edge of the field so that, if the sheep noticed him at all, they would be lulled into a false sense of security, deluded into thinking that it was not they that he was after. He would pass by them harmlessly, thirty or forty yards to one side, sweeping behind them in a pear-shaped arc, to fetch-up at a point from which he could drive them directly to the shepherd, in a straight line through the centre of the Fetch gate in the centre of the course.

In conventional trials, the shepherd is allowed to size up the position of the sheep and the lie of the land so that he can decide whether to send the dog on a left- or right-hand Gather. This would have been difficult to cover on some of the courses used for the Television Trophy because the wonderful scenery often made a better background when viewed from one side or the other. So all the shepherds in a contest were asked to send their dogs to the most photogenic side to gather.

Each dog in the singles of the Television Trophy started off the trial with a total of one hundred points, from which the judges deducted points for each fault scored. (Scoring for conventional trials is slightly different.)

In the Gather or outrun, the commonest faults were not going wide enough on the outrun, or coming up too close behind the sheep and scaring them. If the dog veers too near in or too far out or goes too far past, the shepherd will have to redirect him with a whistle. This may be penalised by docking a mark or

166

half a mark because the judges expect the dog to be sent off in the right direction initially, and to carry on right of his own accord until he stops with the sheep in a direct line between him and the shepherd. If he goes too far past them, he is wasting time; too close and he may startle them and set them off, possibly in the wrong direction. Some sheep will be wilder and more spooky than others, so that there *is* no stereotyped distance behind them for the dog to stop. It is a matter of experience by both man and dog and, if he thinks he's coming in too close, the shepherd can always drop the dog in his tracks by a stop whistle. Ideally, the dog should approach just close enough to alert the sheep, bringing their heads up to watch him without alarming them, but showing enough authority to convince them that he is not to be trifled with. A perfect Gather like this, with no penalties, is worth 20 points.

Sometimes the sheep will tense-up and give the game away that they are likely to move and a clever dog, when that happens, will not stop directly behind them but will overshoot his mark a trifle. Proof of success or failure comes within seconds. The next part of the trial is the Lift, when the sheep take the dog's first command to get moving. They should start directly towards the shepherd and continue, in a dead straight line, towards the centre of the first or Fetch gate. If the dog had sensed the direction they preferred, and overshot his mark slightly to drive home the point that he'd cut them off if they diverged, he obviously will not be in a straight line with the shepherd, the sheep and the centre of the gate. This is not a fault but sophisticated shepherding – and a penalty-free Lift is worth 10 points.

Once they have started, the dog must keep them

going at a steady pace to demonstrate that he is in command. Too fast is bad shepherding, for it sheds off profit; too slow and they will begin to graze so that he will have to get up close and hurry them. The result will be that they will progress by jerky fits-and-starts, losing points as they come. Sheep can be very stubborn about where they will, or will not, go willingly so that if they show signs of digressing, the shepherd will order the dog to left or right to correct it. Any serious kinks in their progress will be penalised by loss of marks.

A perfect Fetch brings the sheep through the middle of the fetch gate directly to the feet of the shepherd, and the dog will make them pass as close to his master as he can – short of splitting the bunch when some go each side; then he will turn them close round the shepherd to begin the next section, which is the Drive.

It is relatively easy to get your dog to bring a bunch of your own sheep close to you and to turn them close round the stake in as tight a hairpin bend as possible. Your sheep know you and trust you because you feed them and minister to their wants. It is a very different thing to get the same bunch to place their trust in a stranger by going within reach of the business end of his shepherd's crook at the end of the Gather.

A perfect Fetch is worth 20 points and, as they make the turn around the shepherd, they set off on the Drive which is the most difficult manoeuvre in the trial. Dogs naturally fetch things to their masters, but it is not natural to drive them away. Once behind the sheep, a dog will turn them to the right automatically if his master moves him to their left and he cannot help driving them away if his master gives the command or whistle 'Walk-on' behind them. So the direction they take at the beginning of the cross-drive is almost entirely up to the shepherd. He should aim them smack in the middle of the cross-drive gates, which is a space seven yards wide.

The moment they are through this gap, they should be turned sharp round to go directly across the course towards the hurdles, or gates, on the other side. It is particularly difficult for the shepherd to assess whether they are on the right line for this cross-drive because, being at right angles to it himself, and a hundred yards away, he has no means of getting behind the dog to get an accurate bearing. Nevertheless, if the sheep weave to right and left, progress erratically or go round the gate instead of through it, the dog will lose points for every fault.

As soon as they negotiate the gate at the other end of the cross-drive, the dog slips round them to turn them towards his master. It is, of course, perfectly legitimate for him to receive necessary commands, either by word or whistle, during the whole of the trial and the shepherd will only lose points for this if the judges believe he has over-commanded his collie. In order to get a tight turn after passing through the hurdles on the cross-drive, the dog usually has to slip round, not through them, so that he is almost waiting for his sheep on the other side to turn them. Over-enthusiasm here will send them back through the gap – which will lose all the points for that obstacle.

It is one of the many places where skill with sheep is equally important as skill at handling dogs, because a clever shepherd will anticipate what a particular bunch of sheep are going to do. He will spot if they are likely to bolt if the dog gets too near, and calculate just how far behind them he must drift him along to maintain a steady but unhurried pace.

After the cross-drive, the 'race' is sometimes used. This is a narrow passage which is more difficult than normal wide gates, and a further refinement is the Maltese Cross in which sheep are driven through the race in two directions.

They should come straight on towards the shepherd and into the sawdust circle of the shedding ring. A perfect cross-drive will notch up another 30 points.

The shedding ring is twenty yards in diameter, half as large as on a conventional National Trials course. From the spectators' point of view, shedding is perhaps the most exciting part of the whole trial. Two of the five sheep have red ribbons round their necks and one of these has to be separated from the rest without any of them leaving the sawdust ring until the separation is complete. (In National Trials, more sheep are ribboned and the unribboned ones shed off.)

The shepherd may not leave his peg until the dog has the sheep in the sawdust shedding ring and, from then on, the rest of the trial is an even more intimate partnership between man and dog. The technique is to get the dog to 'hold-up' the sheep, standing on the opposite side of the flock. If dog or shepherd approaches too close, the sheep will stream between them to one side or the other. If they are careful and close in to precisely the right distance, the sheep won't panic, but will pass between them quite slowly with reasonable gaps between them. The shepherd, who wants one ribboned sheep on its own, allows them to keep moving until the sheep he wants is at the end of the bunch, with some sort of gap between it and its fellows. He points his crook to make it hesitate, and to widen the gap, at the same time indicating to the dog which sheep he wants. Then he snaps out the command 'Come through' or, sometimes, 'Come here', depending on the shepherd, and, as the dog dives through the gap, the singleton spills off one way and the rest explode in the opposite direction, usually outside the sawdust ring.

The job is not done yet. 'Flocking like sheep' is no haphazard phrase for the instinct of an isolated victim to rejoin the flock is almost overwhelming. While the victim and the flock are still facing each other, the dog's task is not deemed complete because the parting may be no more than luck. To prove his dominance the dog must 'wear' his sheep. He must make it turn away from its fellows in token of submission, admitting that the dog could drive it right away in any direction at will.

'Wear' seems an odd term for this manoeuvre, but it may be derived either from the nautical term 'to wear' – when a ship comes about and turns before the wind – or it could be from the more obvious middle English word for sapping strength or wasting away.

When the judges concede that the dog has not only singled a beribboned sheep but demonstrated his dominance by wearing it, they cry, 'That'll do'. Only when the shepherd hears his dog has won approval may he call him to heel and allow the single sheep to rejoin the flock, leaving him 10 points nearer victory for a perfect shed.

All that now remains is to get them in the pen, which is composed of hurdles, and is six feet wide and nine feet deep. One side consists of a hurdle hinged to form a gate, to which is secured a rope six feet long. The shepherd walks straight from the shedding ring to this pen, takes one end of the rope, which he may

171

not let go till the sheep are in the pen. Meanwhile, he sends the dog to collect all five sheep, regrouping them if they are still dispersed after their ordeal in the shedding ring.

To the dog, the pen must look like a toy boat on an ocean. All the room in the world for the sheep to go round it, only six feet to go in. The shepherd is not allowed to help collect and drive them to the pen but he does, of course, control his dog's pace and direction. The vital thing is to keep the sheep well-bunched and neither to rush them nor give them too much time to size up the situation by allowing them to dawdle. They will almost certainly pause at the entrance to the pen, and impatience here may 'burst' them and make them scatter instead of walking into what must to them look like a trap.

At this stage, the shepherd may help his dog. He can stand with crook outstretched away from the pen to make a lead-in funnel on his side. His experience with sheep will let him see inside their minds and forestall evasion by waving his crook or shuffling his feet to distract them at the instant the leader may be deciding to make a dash. The dog is equally capable of matching cunning with cunning. He will crouch, quivering and tense, licking his chops and daring their disobedience with his hypnotic eyes. The whole group, hunters and hunted, may stay suspended between victory and defeat for long seconds at a stretch.

Sometimes the pendulum will swing one way, sometimes the other. If there happens to be an odd ewe out among the bunch, she may make an irrational dash for freedom and disappear round the outside of the pen. Then the dog must go round to retrieve her and the whole patient process starts all over again. This time it will be even harder because, once a sheep makes up her mind not to enter the pen, and tastes success by evading it, she will very likely try it on again – and again – costing half a point or a point each time she succeeds. One of the most interesting rebels to watch is the aggressive old ewe which, deciding that enough is enough, turns round to face the dog and see him off.

People who have nothing to do with sheep may think they are harmless, cuddly old creatures. How wrong they are. Many years ago, I reared a cade lamb on the bottle to cure a bull terrier I had of false ideas that sheep came in the same quarry category as rats. By the time the lamb weighed about forty pounds – the same weight as the dog – it was intensely playful, and its idea of a game was to put its head down and charge at whatever it considered to be a potential playmate.

The term battering ram for an instrument designed to drive wooden piles into the solid earth was obviously coined by a countryman well versed in the ways of sheep. My cade lamb would wait till the dog was not looking, roll his eyes and launch himself into the attack, delivering a rib-shattering blow when he collided, which sent the dog spinning head-over-heels for yards. As I did not allow the dog to retaliate, it took very little of such medicine to convince him to treat anything with wool on with respect. If I had connived, of course, he would have gone in and killed it in revenge.

The lamb finally wrote out the recipe for his own mint sauce, however. Jess happened to be looking the other way when he chose her for his target, practically putting her in orbit. It was a fatal charge!

If a dog is unlucky enough to get such a brute in the bunch he is trying to pen, it lays open his courage to be tested while everyone is watching. The culprit is usually an old ewe which turns her back on the pen, stamps her foot and dares her opponent to advance. Some dogs, having tasted the medicine that cured my bull terrier, will turn tail and retreat, which costs them points for cowardice. The best dogs just back away and bare their fangs. If the sheep won't take 'No' for an answer, the dog will discipline her by biting her on the nose. It is the only form of gripping which is not penalised in a trial because the dog is expected to be in control at all times and there is only one answer for such insubordination.

The snag is that once having tasted the sweets of unbridled power, the dog can't help but yearn for more. The temptation to grip, not at the business end of an attacking ewe, but on the haunches of a compliant one, is sometimes overwhelming and dogs that savage sheep's backsides are soon disqualified.

It is always a difficult decision whether to err on the side of a 'sharp' dog which might grip, or a softer dog which might not stop a bolter. Sheep themselves vary, not only with breeds, some of which are wilder and more headstrong than others, but according to season since ewes are far tougher to handle when they have lambs. So a dog that is just right for the bunch of sheep at one trial may be either too hard or soft for the sheep at the next. It is this element of luck with the sheep and the way they behave that takes all certainty out of predicting even the most skilful man as winner.

Sooner or later, the job is done with varying success, depending on skill and hazard. If all goes well, the sheep are gathered, lifted, fetched and driven with fewer lost points than any of their rivals. Reluctant ribboned ewes are orphaned from their fellows, reunited and then popped safely in the pen to leave the man and his dog a total of a hundred unsullied points.

However good the run, there are always near squeaks and apprehensions. No two runs are the same, no two dogs are equal. Good shepherds are sometimes weak on dog work and marvellous handlers not so hot on sheep. Every day that I watched, I appreciated more fine points that had passed over my head before. I made new friends within the sheepdog world and began to appreciate that sheep had more courage than I thought and even the wisest dogs surprised me by their cunning.

The snag was that when they left off, it was my turn to begin. Philip left what he called topping and tailing the programme till 'what mattered'(!) was in the bag. The fact that my stuff *didn't* matter did not mean that he did not expect it to be put together well.

'Topping' meant introducing the programme. Simple enough, in theory. All I had to do was to say where we were, paint an atmospheric word picture, and give a preview of what the customers could hope to see. I had to explain, live to camera, that the first rounds would be the national teams, competing amongst themselves, to decide who would go forward to represent his country as National champion in the semi-finals, and in the final to decide the International champion.

'Tailing' the programme consisted of announcing who had won and, usually, talking to the winner, or doing a piece with Eric Halsall who did not appear so often in front of camera, so that viewers could put a face to his voice in the commentary.

Some of these pieces were quite difficult to do naturally. It feels odd to talk to an impersonal camera,

175

stuck halfway up a mountain, half a mile from your producer. The camera has been there all day, pouching birds'-eye views of the competitors. An uncomfortable but photogenic boulder has been chosen to allow the wretched front man to perch precarious, half-way between earth and heaven, so that the camera sees him picked out against the towering crags. In this battle with unstable equilibrium, I am expected to give an evocative impression of the scene some hidden camera sees.

But which scene? There is one camera perched on high by the Simon Truck. His field of view encompasses the neat-laid trials course with an artist's plan of Eric's geometric obstacles. Or, if he swings through ninety degrees, he floods his view with the azure waters of the lake or, by raising his sights, feasts on trim farmsteads, wallowing in prosperity from well-fed sheep and well-fleeced tourists. I can talk to him, because he hears what I say over the radio microphone pinned to my tie. But I can't hear what he says, so I have to use Gerry and her walkie-talkie as my ears. So I ask her to enquire what Philip hopes to have on his master screen at the time he is hearing the introduction from me.

He says he doesn't know! There is rather a dramatic cloud, drifting into position at the head of the valley. Would I like to do a piece about the kaleidoscopic light and shades? I am asked. Or what about the cattle grazing in the paddock by the farm? Perhaps their tranquillity might set the mood. My job is to tailor words to fit whatever view his best picture dictates at the time he is ready to shoot.

After three or four minutes perched on my minuscule proscenium jutting from the hillside, my backside is wet and cramp in the back of my legs knots-up my concentration into inextricable confusion. I am painfully aware that it would be all too easy to suffer my worst of all nightmares, a broadcaster's blank. There is always the possibility of falling into a mental abyss, when all words fail at the critical moment.

So far, more by luck than judgment perhaps, it has never happened to me. But I was once in a programme that was broadcast live, when a man not only forgot completely what he had been going to say – but he couldn't even remember his own name. Yet, till the camera started rolling, he was positively flatulent with over-confidence. I break out into a cold sweat for him every time I think of it.

As things turned out, all went reasonably well. Philip is so unflappable that he can inspire confidence in others and encourage the best out of them whether the going is rough or smooth. When I wanted to concentrate on the femininity of rounded hills, he brought them up in silhouettes like some prehistoric bathing belle, spread-eagled across the horizon. In that wild countryside, there is always something fresh; something exciting or amusing – or as rare as when I had the luck to spot an eagle, soaring majestically overhead, as if he'd drifted down from the Scottish border especially to watch the trials.

One day the fell hounds streamed along the rugged mountain above us, screaming hate and destruction to the long-legged fox that had played hell with the lambs a few months before. There was the intricate maze of stone walls to look at, high enough to keep even hill sheep where they were wanted, but with the subsidiary purpose of improving the grazing inside the area they encompassed. Our ancestors had probably picked the stones off their fields, because grass can't grow when its covered by a rock. Once they had collected them, they had the choice of sterilising more land by stacking them in useless cairns or building them into walls to do positive good.

Philip's topping and tailing bits did not give scope to go into much detail because Time is master in his trade and his purpose was to show sheepdogs, not to launch me into a diatribe on the history of agriculture. But he didn't mind a bit of verbal colour and he allowed me a minute a time, or one minute and fifteen seconds when he was feeling generous. To concoct anything cohesive off the cuff is not as easy as you might think. And to seal it into seventy-five seconds was stringent verbal discipline.

My worry at the beginning of the series was that when we had seen one trial, we would have seen them all. One gather would look like another gather, and a cross-drive would be a cross-drive whether the sheep behaved or not. I am glad that I was wrong. Not only did I become involved personally with the competitive aspect and rooted for the chaps and dogs that I liked best, but I found the competitors delightful in their own right.

Mervyn Williams, for example, is a farmer from Kington in Herefordshire. He farms getting on for three hundred acres in-bye land with his brother, and they have spent their whole lives on the land they work, which also includes hill grazing in Radnorshire.

Like so many such countrymen, he exudes the quiet, unassuming confidence of men who have always been their own masters and monarchs of the land they farm. And well he might, because he has run dogs in trials for thirty years and been in international teams eight times. So he had nothing to worry about. But, before it was his turn to run, I noticed him pacing up and down like a tiger in a cage. I sidled up, talked to him of sheep and dogs, but his eyes had a faraway look and it was obvious that he was making polite conversation mechanically, so I made myself scarce and left him to it.

He did a copy-book run so, when it was all over, we talked again and this time he confided that before a trial he gets so steamed-up that he has to go away and sweat it out himself or he might transmit his mental jitters to his dog. I confessed that I am much the same except that it is after it is over that I am at my worst. I find it difficult to wind-down at night so that, by about Thursday of the week when we are recording *One Man and His Dog*, I don't get off to sleep at all. It's then a question of living on my nerves till an outsize slug of alcohol at the party we have on the last night sends me to bed ready to go out like a light. He seemed pleased to discover that his complaint was not unique.

How folk like Philip stand the strain is quite beyond me. Instead of having to worry about a few odd bits of topping and tailing or interviewing nice people about pleasant subjects they know inside out, the whole spectrum of responsibility falls on his shoulders. The moment he has finished one pro-gramme, he pitches himself straight into the next, and the intricacy of the homework he does for each would pile most people's workload high for months on end.

In some ways, his job must have been the most frustrating of all when a trial was being run. We could see whatever we wanted to see. We could look back across the field to be impressed by the size of the enterprise; we could creep into the judges' tent to see if they were bickering about their decisions or join the spectators to see things from their point of view.

179

Philip was locked up in the scanner, limited in what he could see to the second-hand images regurgitated onto his little screens by his cameras.

He had to wait till the judges had decided which dog had won – the result was relayed to him via the stage manager on the field telephone – before he could tell Andy Bloomfield, who then punched up the correct figures for Philip to superimpose on the picture of the shepherd and his dog who waited by the pen of sheep until told to move off.

Philip could punch up the picture of the winning shepherd (with his points in a corner of the screen) and then mix to whatever picture he wanted by pressing the right button at the right time.

When I got the chance to steal into the scanner and curl up in comfort in a corner, I watched the whole sophisticated process open-mouthed. A logical, cohesive narrative was conjured out of separate continuous pictures as if the whole operation was simple. The more I watched, the more I marvelled at such an exhibition of sustained concentration.

One of the most pleasant interludes was the Irish Heats in the second series. The competitors were not only as good as anyone else, they had the spark of originality one expects from the Emerald Isle. Tim Flood turned up with his bizarre nose whistle, on which he could play soft Irish airs as well as command his dog. He got a lively bunch of sheep which, combined with his dog's enthusiasm, went through the obstacles all right, but at ever increasing pace till they disappeared in a hustle in the car park. Tim retrieved them impeccably – at the cost of a few penalty points – and we were quietly, if unkindly, pleased because we had been slightly worried that the standard was so high that it might give viewers the false impression that the whole thing was easy. The spectacle of a bunch of cunning old ewes disappearing without trace came, we felt, at just the right time.

There is no accounting for taste. When the audience research figures were issued for that programme we were astonished to find that it had not been enjoyed as much as usual. Viewers proved us wrong by telling us that we had failed to show them such a high standard of dogs!

I am delighted to say that Martin O'Neill wiped their eye for them by beating all comers and winning the Television Singles Trophy for Ireland. He is a tall softly spoken Irishman from County Meath who has been a shepherd all his life, and represented Ireland six times in international competition. In spite of a stroppy old ewe who didn't like the rest of the sheep, he gave a delightfully relaxed exhibition of working sheep with dogs. When it was done and I went up to chat with him, he told me with his infectious Irish smile. "Tis is the best day of me loife, I never t'ought I could win in sich company!' Although his slow soft brogue matched the gentle misty colours of his native land, his mind was sharp and crisp so that there had been no doubt throughout that he could keep a mental step – or two! – ahead of the most determined woolly rebel in his flock.

His wife had come over to watch him, so when we had finished the interview, I went over to congratulate her too. 'I expect you're very proud of him?' I asked.

'Oi am, that,' she said, 'in spoite of the fact that he t'ought the world of me last week – and oi know the dog will be foist in his mind now!'

Martin O'Neill had the greatest bad luck, the following week, not to win the Singles Champion of

Champions against the winner from the previous year. For one thing, the dog which had won the year before was ill and the replacement put one sheep outside a gate on the cross-drive.

So we thought that all Martin had to do was to get all his sheep through all the obstacles – and he couldn't fail to win. But he was fated again with a stroppy old ewe who kept trying to wander off course, making the others digress a little from the straight line.

The judges eventually decided that more points were lost by not keeping the line direct than by putting a sheep the wrong side of the gate, making Martin lose by a whisker.

It was a bit of a comedown after such exhibitions to have to get down to routine work myself. For one of these capers, Philip had picked a background of solid grey stone barns, merging into lush grazing in the foothills beyond. He wanted me to stand up, look into the camera lens as if it were my best friend's eyes, and spiel off a string of attractions which were promised for the subsequent programme.

There had been quite a gap between the end of the trial and my job of work, so Geoff Lomas had re-sited a camera and sound engineer complete with their accoutrements. So there, in the centre of nowhere, was quite an array of photographic armaments, obviously set up for immediate use.

A gaggle of hikers hove into view and, according to their custom, they gathered round with boundless curiosity. I was set up on my mark about five yards from the camera and left to cool my heels for quite a while. The gapers gawped and fired loud questions at each other in the obvious hope that someone knowledgeable would answer. They got no takers.

Meanwhile Philip had had the camera trained on me without liking what he saw. My head was too low in relation to the background, so Geoff sent someone to fetch a packing-case. Still too low but, as the whole conversation was carried out over the walkie-talkie, I was kept in ignorance of what was wrong or what remedy was proposed. I only found out when another packing-case was brought and stood on top of the other. Then I was bundled onto the top of that so that I towered above the crowd like Guy Fawkes on his bonfire.

The hikers were fascinated, as I could hear from their speculations. I got the impression that some imagined an invisible gibbet above my head so that I could be pushed off my platform to swing twixt heaven and earth, a macabre warning to all who muff their lines. Such processes drag on interminably, and I had to repeat my spiel several times before sound and picture were all to Philip's satisfaction. Each time I went over the same ground a lady, just behind the camera, elbowed her pneumatic neighbour to say, "'E's just said that, duck. Can't they hear him?'

Standing on such a platform, in the middle of no-where, with a broken arm, before such an audience is not calculated to inflate self-confidence! Andy encapsulated the incident by producing, in the bar that night, a wicked cartoon of a portly fellow wearing a cap and with arm in a sling, standing on a soap box, surrounded only by a bunch of sheep.

The caption says, 'So this is what being on the box is'!

The most spectacular part of the whole trials were the competitions between pairs of dogs running as a brace. It seems clever enough to most people, who probably daren't let their own brutes off a lead in public, when a shepherd can direct his dog from several hundred yards away. That he can do this with two dogs, each obeying a quite different code of commands, seems little short of miraculous.

These Brace Trials not only entail a differently designed course, but different procedures as well. Instead of the usual bunch of five sheep being turned out of the pen at the top of the field, six appear and are coaxed as near to the central peg as possible.

The shepherd stands at his mark in front of the judges' tent, with one dog sitting on each side of him and, on the signal to start, he sends one on the outrun to one side of the field, and the other dog to the other. Each must run wide and swing-in towards the other, in the usual pear-shaped arc, to fetch-up well behind the sheep at the top of the field. If, in so doing, they cross each other's path, they must remain for the rest of the trial to the side on which they finished the outrun. They must not change sides again. If, on the other hand, they do not cross, but finish up on the sides they started, they must remain there, without changing sides at all. A perfect Gather will earn them 10 points apiece.

Their next task is to lift the sheep, or start them moving, and bring them in the same straight line as a single drive, through the central gate, round the shepherd, round the triangular cross-drive course and back to the sawdust shedding ring. To avoid notching penalties, each dog must do his share, though one can be driving behind and the other sneaking ahead to help obtain a perfect turn. The maximum points are 20 each for Lift, Fetch and Drive.

There is no jealousy like professional jealousy – and dogs are no exception. Some dogs bear each other an implacable hatred and cannot bear to share their triumph with another, or even allow him to come within yards of their beloved boss. Since he is boss of both, this can lead to moments so awkward that it is impossible to work some of the best dogs together as a brace.

Some dogs grow so jealous that they have to be tied up apart at home and Glyn Jones actually sold a wonderful dog because such a feud flared up between it and his much-loved champion, Gel, that he feared they would do each other mortal injury if either got loose and went to the other's kennel. Ironically, Gel strained a leg soon after and was in plaster for several weeks so that he missed a lot of trials Glyn *might* have won with the dog he had sold.

If, however, all goes well in the brace trial, the six sheep in the shedding ring have to be divided into two bunches of three instead of the one beribboned one being shed off. Either dog may do this task with help from the shepherd and his waving crook as in an ordinary singles shed. In neither case is he allowed to help to the extent of actually touching a sheep. At some trials, bunches of sheep are ten or even twenty.

Instead of one pen to put them in, there are two on the brace course, neither of which has a gate that can be closed by pulling a rope. The pen consists instead of a simple three-sided hurdle enclosure with an entrance five feet wide. The dog that gets the first three into this pen is then responsible for keeping them there, while his boss goes off with his partner and the other three sheep. These are driven to another, similar, pen on the other side of the field. In one series we used a Land-Rover and trailer.

The temptation for the dog acting custodian to leave his lot in the pen and dash over to help the boss with the other lot is almost insurmountable. Even the best dogs may glance over their shoulders or turn their backs on their captives to assure themselves that all goes well. Occasionally, one will shuffle a little nearer the boss – and further from the sheep – until they make a dash to join the rest of the bunch, spoiling both attempts at penning. But, if things run smoothly, the first dog will keep his charges under tight restraint while the other dog and his boss pop the remainder in the second pen and notch-up a maximum score of 20 points for the penning.

Glyn Jones is a past master at this art and he won the Brace Championship in the first series convincingly. So he was invited back, to battle it out with Tot Longton, the winner of the Brace Championship in the second series, for the title of Champion of Champions.

Tot is Tim Longton's brother, and is also steeped in generations of the blood of sheep farmers and their working collies. He has no less than nine English Brace Championships and one International under his belt. In the brace trials in the second series though, Tot had a shaky start because he was running Jed and Kerry, the one very experienced and the other, by these standards, something of a novice. It showed up. The old dog – and his boss! – did superbly by winning the Brace although the youngster nearly let them down. They scraped home the winners but, against Glyn in the Champion of Champions, there was no comparison. Tot's young dog had acquired the polish of a seasoned performer and I couldn't understand the magic transformation.

It was a classic example of a clever handler winning a trial in spite of – and not because of – his dog. All he had done to work an apparent miracle was to swap them over so that the right-hand dog ran on the left next time and vice versa! Like people, some dogs are naturally left-handed and others right.

However unbiased one tries to be, it would be difficult to become as involved with Glyn as I had, in filming the training of his puppy Glen, without wishing him all the luck there was in the battle for the title of Champion of Champions. He didn't need it, for his virtuoso performance with his English- and Welsh-speaking dogs was practically unbeatable and announcing the fact was one of my most pleasant tasks.

Eric, during all this time, had been anything but idle. He spent the whole of every trial, in every series, behind the judges' table near the judges' tent. This was a little unconventional because outsiders are not normally allowed near enough to hear what judges say while they are discussing which dog to nominate as winner.

The reason for Eric's presence is that judging is a subjective exercise and it is often a matter of personal opinion which dog runs out the winner. Eric, an international judge himself, was to be the expert, explaining to viewers not only which dog had won – which could be seen from the marks in the caption – but also why. So it was vital that he gave a fair assessment of the judges' marking without interjecting personal opinions, which might have been conflicting.

For each trial he started with an unmarked plan of the course and, as the trial developed, he plotted in the precise route that was taken by the sheep. Every deviation was there for all to see; his notes marked clearly where a dog had boobed or where a sheep had gone round instead of through an obstacle. Each stage of the trial was marked on his plan with the number of points the judges had awarded. He overheard what they said – and asked, when he didn't – so that, when the trial was over, his plan clearly showed what happened, and why.

If a trial took longer than there was time to show in its entirety, Eric could then tell Philip exactly where the crises occurred, so preventing any chance of editing-out some critical bit and making a nonsense of the result. Months later, when we went to Shepherd's Bush to add commentary to silent film, the annotated plans that Eric had done at the time gave him such total recall that he could produce authoritative commentary which resurrected the spontaneous excitement he had felt at the time.

When the competitions were over, Glyn Jones returned to make another bow. So many viewers had been fascinated by watching him training Glen that Philip had invited him to bring along the puppy and give him a spin round the real trials course.

It is one thing to put a puppy through his paces on home ground but to bring him out in front of such distinguished company is quite another. I hadn't seen him for several weeks but I know Glyn well enough to realise that he wouldn't have brought him without being confident he'd put up a good show. Philip asked the judges to let him go round without bothering to allot marks, but I had become so involved that I probably felt as nervous as Glyn and all the viewers who had expressed such delight in watching his training.

We needn't have bothered. Glen went round the course like an old stager, never putting a foot wrong. If he had been awarded marks, there was many an international-class dog around the ring which would have hung his head. Glen got a fan mail that would not have disgraced a pop star!

When the dust had long settled on the first series, Philip telephoned, out of the blue, to invite Eric and me to a party where the British Academy Awards were to be presented. The British Academy of Film and Television Arts was formed by an amalgamation of the British Film Academy and the Guild of Television Producers and Directors.

Outstanding programmes, by both BBC and ITV are nominated annually and grouped into categories, ranging from the Best Light Entertainment or Drama to the Best Specialist Programme or Outside Broadcast. These nominations are made by professionals and judged on their merits by juries of professionals and it is a great distinction even to be nominated.

We were delighted for Philip, when we discovered that *One Man and His Dog* had got into the final five in the category for Best Specialist Programme. The ceremony was to be televised, including an excerpt from our programme, but nobody would know who had come first until Princess Anne made the presentation. Philip was eventually just pipped for the award but it was a great thrill to be there when his work was publicly recognised.

We returned to the table to make a night of it and teased Gerry, whose name had appeared on the credit titles as Geraldine Cole. We decided that, in future, she must be known as The Hon., with a huge H aspirate, since no title less prestigious would seem nearly posh enough!

Eric surfaced, from time to time, through purple clouds of smoke, to stuff the Head of Events and Entertainments Programmes' head with sheepdog epics of the past, while Philip schemed of epics he would yet produce.

It was the most memorable of many happy evenings and was followed, some weeks later, by another token, in a minor key, that has also meant a lot.

Jess and I had taken a rare day off to visit an old friend, who is a Chief Forester in the Lake District. We spent a glorious day, relaxing in the solitude of his forest, watching roe deer and birds and discussing his plans for improving the area for wildlife as well as for the production of trees.

When we returned to the local, comfortably thirsty and weary, a complete stranger approached. 'I'm Fred Prickett,' he said. 'I heard you were coming and, as I have enjoyed the sheepdog programmes so much, I thought I'd make you this.'

'This' was a magnificent hand-carved shepherd's crook. It is a hazel stick, crowned by the horn of a noble Herdwick ram. Fred Prickett had spent scores of hours carving it, not for profit nor for pride, but simply as a countryman's thanks for something he'd enjoyed.

Out of that solid horn, he's fashioned a handsome sheepdog, one ear cocked as he watches three sheep. There is no doubt about his strength of eye because they've never moved a muscle since I've had the crook. When the unseen shepherd gives the word, that dog will drive them into the perfect hurdle pen, carved on the opposite side of the handle. It is a superb piece of craftsmanship, as intricate as the ancient art of herding sheep.

What a delightful compliment, not only for Philip and his team, but also for every dog and shepherd who made the series possible.

I know of no nicer way of saying 'That'll do!'

Two more books by Phil Drabble on his
Country Life, also available from Sphere

Phil Drabble's Country Scene

Phil Drabble's life is a dream come true. Frustrated
by the artificial existence of industrialised society,
he made the decision to escape to a countryside haven,
where he now enjoys the peace and satisfaction
of rural living.

From bashful badgers to bats in the belfry,
COUNTRY SCENE is an endlessly absorbing
chronicle of a way of life that, sadly, is now rare.

"A diary that is down to earth and full of shrewd
comment about his world and what goes on in it."

Country Life

Country Seasons

Phil Drabble is a true countryman. From his
Staffordshire home, he has lived in close harmony with
the wildlife of the woods and fields.

In this book he takes us through a full year's cycle
of country seasons and introduces us to some of the
creatures, wild and tame, that share his life.
Observant, humorous, fascinatingly informative,
COUNTRY SEASONS will delight town – and
country – dweller alike.

"A rare treat for those who may be compelled to live
through duller seasons in less beautiful surroundings."

Country Life

All Sphere Books are available at your bookshop or
newsagent, or can be ordered from the following address:
Sphere Books, Cash Sales Department,
P.O. Box 11, Falmouth, Cornwall.

Please send cheque or postal order (no currency), and allow
19p for postage and packing for the first book plus 9p
per copy for each additional book ordered up to a
maximum charge of 73p in U.K.

Customers in Eire and B.F.P.O. please allow 19p for
postage and packing for the first book plus 9p per copy
for the next 6 books, thereafter 3p per book.

Overseas customers please allow 20p for postage and
packing for the first book and 10p per copy for each
additional book.